UNIVERSITY OF NORTH CAROLINA AT CHAPEL HILL
DEPARTMENT OF ROMANCE LANGUAGES

NORTH CAROLINA STUDIES
IN THE ROMANCE LANGUAGES AND LITERATURES

*Founder:* URBAN TIGNER HOLMES

*Distributed by:*

UNIVERSITY OF NORTH CAROLINA PRESS
CHAPEL HILL
North Carolina 27514
U.S.A.

NORTH CAROLINA STUDIES IN THE
ROMANCE LANGUAGES AND LITERATURES

Number 201

# TECHNIQUES OF IRONY IN ANATOLE FRANCE

### ESSAY ON *LES SEPT FEMMES DE LA BARBE-BLEUE*

# TECHNIQUES OF IRONY IN ANATOLE FRANCE

ESSAY ON
*LES SEPT FEMMES DE LA BARBE-BLEUE*

BY

DIANE WOLFE LEVY

CHAPEL HILL

NORTH CAROLINA STUDIES IN THE ROMANCE
LANGUAGES AND LITERATURES
U.N.C. DEPARTMENT OF ROMANCE LANGUAGES
1978

Library of Congress Cataloging in Publication Data

Levy, Diane Wolfe.
   Techniques of irony in Anatole France.

   (North Carolina studies in the Romance languages and literatures; no. 201)
   Bibliography: p.
   1. France, Anatole, 1844-1924. Les sept femmes de la Barbe-Bleue. 2. Irony in literature. I. Title. II. Series.

PQ2254.S434        843'.8        78-18827
ISBN 0-8078-9201-7

I. S. B. N. 0-8078-9201-7

DEPÓSITO LEGAL: V. 1.833 - 1978        I. S. B. N. 84-399-8514-2
ARTES GRÁFICAS SOLER, S. A. - JÁVEA, 28 - VALENCIA (8) - 1978

# TABLE OF CONTENTS

|  | Page |
|---|---|
| INTRODUCTION | 9 |
| I. "LES SEPT FEMMES DE LA BARBE-BLEUE" | 21 |
| II. "LE GRAND SAINT NICOLAS" | 52 |
| III. "L'HISTOIRE DE LA DUCHESSE DE CICOGNE ET DE M. DE BOULINGRIN QUI DORMIRENT CENT ANS EN COMPAGNIE DE LA BELLE AU BOIS DORMANT" | 79 |
| IV. "LA CHEMISE" | 107 |
| CONCLUSION | 142 |
| APPENDIX | 145 |
| SELECTED BIBLIOGRAPHY | 160 |

# INTRODUCTION

Anatole France was a master story-teller, and his short stories rank among his best-known and most interesting works. If the short story form imposes certain restrictions, it can also result in a refinement and condensation of both thought and technique. France's ironic and detached manner and his careful craftmanship appear at their best in this showcase genre.

The story generally accepted as France's *chef d'œuvre*[1] is "Le Procurateur de Judée," published in 1892 in *L'Etui de Nacre*. Apparently artless yet meticulously calculated, this story is constructed as an organic whole with no extraneous details; or rather, whose every detail contributes to its central meaning. This total concentration of focus has been called the "aesthetic secret" of France's most successful short stories.[2] More specifically, "Le Procurateur de Judée" is typically Francian in both structure and thematic concerns. Its effect rests on a "brilliantly prepared ending which is both inevitably natural and yet a surprise, and endless ironic reverberations which the story sets up in the reader at its end, raising questions about the relativity of historical truth, fame, and religious faith, and about our perception of the past."[3]

It is ironic that France's masterpiece should prove a poor model for other stories. The surprise ending, when expected, ceases to

---

[1] See Murray Sachs, *Anatole France: The Short Stories* (Southampton: The Camelot Press Ltd., 1974), a perceptive study of France's personal "discovery" and mastery of the genre and its importance in his *œuvre*. The Sachs monograph, which appeared during the final revisions of this manuscript, announces a recrudescence of critical interest in France, an author whose work offers much opportunity for further stylistic analysis.
[2] Sachs, Op. cit., p. 42.
[3] *Ibid.*

be a surprise, no matter how perfect the technique. While remaining faithful to his aesthetic of concentrated focus, then, France would go on to develop different narrative techniques in the best of his subsequent stories. In "Crainquebille" and "Riquet" (1904) for example, the narration takes the point of view of an "innocent" protagonist, thus flattering the superior perception of the reader. And in *Les Sept Femmes de la Barbe-Bleue et autres contes merveilleux* (1909), the last of his eight collections of short stories,[4] France uses a complex system of parody to provide the reader with constant and often paradoxical surprises throughout the text, rather than laying a final literary ambush.

*Les Sept Femmes de la Barbe-Bleue* reiterates France's life-long concern with history and epistemology, and returns to the legendary, supernatural, and religious themes he so often used throughout his career. Religious or supernatural figures are central to *Thaïs, L'Ile des Pingouins, La Révolte des anges,* and many of the stories included in *L'Etui de nacre, Le Puits de Sainte Claire, Les Contes de Jacques Tournebroche,* and of course, *Les Sept Femmes de la Barbe-Bleue.*

Like the hapless M. Fulgence Tapir, deluged by facts in the preface to *L'Ile des Pingouins,* one is tempted to murmer "Que d'art!" when faced with the scope of France's familiarity with art, architecture, and literature. He has aptly been called a modern polyhistor,[5] for his interests were as widespread as they were eccentric, and they are reflected throughout his own works. France was particularly fond of the traditional stories and legends which he considered a valuable part of his country's cultural heritage. Songs, stories, sermons, saints' lives — he examined each new scholarly edition and often the original manuscripts. France was a voracious reader, and as literary critic for *Le Temps* (from 1886 to 1892) he had ample opportunity to pursue his varied interests in his weekly articles. His knowledge of legends and folklore can

---

[4] *Le Puits de Sainte Claire* (1895); *Balthasar* (1889); *Clio* (1900); *L'Etui de Nacre* (1902); *Crainquebille, Riquet et plusieurs autres récits* (1904); *Sur la Pierre Blanche* (1905); *Les Contes de Jacques Tournebroche* (1908).

[5] Dushan Bresky, *The Art of Anatole France* (Paris and The Hague: Mouton, 1969), p. 207.

be seen in the many discussions of these topics in the articles collected in *La Vie Littéraire*.[6]

An even earlier indication of France's predilection for traditional tales is found in his "Dialogue sur les contes de fées" (first published in 1885 in *La Suisse Romande* and included later that year in France's *Le Livre de mon ami*). The *Dialogue* reveals France's expertise in mythological exegesis and his familiarity with the pioneering figures in folklore: Baron Walckenaer, Alfred Maury, Max Müller. But the *Dialogue* is primarily a sincere plea for treasuring fairy tales as they are, without destroying their charm by needless commentary. He finds the naïve simplicity of folktales charming; indeed, "S'ils n'étaient pas absurdes, ils ne seraient pas charmants."[7] The origin of the tales is irrelevant to France; what matters is the emotional need these stories fulfill:

> Il faut des contes aux petits et aux grands enfants, de beaux contes en vers ou en prose, des écrits qui nous donnent à rire ou à pleurer, et qui nous mettent dans l'enchantement.[8]

However, when France returns to the same tales many years later in *Les Sept Femmes de la Barbe-Bleue,* his emphasis is entirely different. His point here is not that historical commentary is irrelevant but that it is impossible. The scientific historical method is the butt of his satire, and the fairy tale or folk legend, far from the cherished childhood memory, is taken as the measure of unreliability. The subject may be the same, but the style and focus of the composition are considerably altered. It is true that one hears echoes of other voices and previous tales in these stories.[9] This is not necessarily a weakness, but rather an indication of France's need to rethink, rework, and refine certain ideas.

The reasons for this sharpening of focus and of wit have been discussed at length. Jean Levaillant has analysed France's develop-

---

[6] See e.g. France's review of Gaston Paris (*Œuvres*, VI, 570 ff.); his review of Sébillot, Bladé and others (*Œuvres*, VII, 451 ff.); or the discussion of art and archeology in *Pierre Nozière* (*Œuvres*, X, 430-35).

[7] France, *Le Livre de mon ami*, *Œuvres* (Paris: Calmann-Lévy, 1926), III, 407. Hereafter cited as *Ami*, III.

[8] *Ibid.*, 400.

[9] See Sachs, *Op. cit.*, pp. 44-45.

ing skepticism and the ironic vision of the world which obliged him to engage in "causes" even though he had little confidence in any lasting or positive results. Ever since 1886, France had been gathering material and working on his history of Joan of Arc, and as the work progressed he became more and more fascinated with history itself, "multiple et confuse." [10]

History and historians were often the subject of his literary *causeries* in *Le Temps*. France realized how subjective the selection of historical facts must be:

> Or, comment l'historien juge-t-il qu'un fait est notable ou non? Il en juge arbitrairement, selon son goût et son caprice, à son idée, en artiste enfin! car les faits ne se divisent pas, de leur propre nature, en faits historiques et en faits non historiques. Mais un fait est quelque chose d'extrêmement complexe. L'historien représentera-t-il les faits dans leur complexité? Non, cela est impossible. Il les représentera dénués de la plupart des particularités, mutilés, différents de ce qu'ils furent. Quant aux rapports des faits entre eux, n'en parlons pas. [11]

This overwhelming complexity results in the relativity of all historical interpretation and the futility of establishing order or sequence of cause and effect in the continuum of human events. Standardization or increased rigorousness of method held little promise for France. The most one could expect would be that man's errors would become more scientific as science progressed. [12]

Meanwhile, France demonstrated in his weekly column that history abounds in errors and that any claim at precision is laughable. He gives the exact dates of St. Anthony's life, but adds that their validity would be as miraculous as any of that saint's

---

[10] Jean Levaillant, *Les Aventures du scepticisme: essai sur l'évolution intellectuelle d'Anatole France* (Paris: Armand Colin, 1965), p. 650. Hereafter cited as *Essai*.

[11] France, *La Vie littéraire II* (Paris: Calmann-Lévy, 1926), *Œuvres*, VI, 438-39. France's discussions of history in *La Vie littéraire* are taken from his *Le Jardin d'Epicure* (IX, 458), published in 1894. Moreover, this is exactly how the narrator of France's "L'histoire de la duchesse de Cicogne et de M. de Boulingrin" selects his facts: "Je me propose de communiquer au public ce qui, dans ces révélations, m'a paru le plus intéressant." (France, *Les Sept Femmes de la Barbe-Bleue*, XIX, 217.)

[12] France, *La Vie littéraire I*, VI, 115.

good works; he cites the last words of the Emperor Julian, but adds that "Il n'est pas probable que Julien les ait prononcées telle que l'historien les rapporte, et le discours est peut-être entièrement supposé." [13]

France did not value history for any absolute, factual contribution to the sum of human knowledge. He considered it an art rather than a science, whose sole value lay in its beauty:

> La vieille histoire est un art; c'est pourquoi elle a, dans sa beauté, une vérité spirituelle et idéale bien supérieure à toutes les vérités matérielles et tangibles des sciences d'observation pure: elle peint l'homme et les passions de l'homme. C'est ce que la statistique ne fera jamais. L'histoire narrative est inexacte par essence. Je l'ai dit et ne m'en dédis pas: mais elle est encore, avec la poésie, la plus fidèle image que l'homme ait tracée de lui-même. Elle est un portrait. Votre histoire statistique ne sera jamais qu'une autopsie. [14]

This skepticism with regard to history's accuracy combined with an appreciation of its symbolic grandeur can be seen in *Clio*, a small volume of five short stories published in 1900. As the title indicates, all are inspired by the Muse of History. In them, France elaborates his oblique view of history, focusing on an incidental anecdote (as in "La Muiron") or an historical fact seen from an unusual viewpoint (the "bas bout de la table" in "Le Roi Boit") in order to illuminate one of the many facets of the human side of the past. The two most prominent stories in the collection emphasize spiritual values rather than facts. The historical background of "Le Chanteur de Kymé" is of interest because of the light it sheds on the creative spirit and the role of the artist, unappreciated by his contemporaries as well as the reader who is unaware, until

---

[13] *Ibid.*, 528; *La Vie littéraire IV* (Paris: Calmann-Lévy, 1926), VII, 628.

[14] France, *La Vie littéraire IV*, VII, 445. France repeats this notion in *L'Ile des Pingouins:* "Le présent ouvrage appartient, je dois le reconnaître, au genre de la vieille histoire, de celle qui présente la suite des événements dont le souvenir s'est conservé, et qui indique, autant que possible, les causes et les effets; ce qui est un art plutôt qu'une science. On prétend que cette manière de faire ne contente plus les esprits exacts et que l'antique Clio passe aujourd'hui pour une diseuse de sornettes." (France, *L'Ile des Pingouins*, XVIII, 8.)

the last sentence, that the aged bard of the story is Homer. And in "Komm l'Atrébate," history remains an overwhelming and incomprehensible force, crushing individual action or resistance.

The same pessimistic admiration was expressed in the work he considered his greatest, *La Vie de Jeanne d'Arc* (1908). France replaces the legend of Saint Joan with a story of human courage, weakness, and fanaticism. The second volume, in particular, is marked by bitterness; France's experience with the Dreyfus trial had made him sensitive to the frustrating way in which all great causes can be hampered by the contingencies of everyday life, and this experience colored his analysis of Joan's trial. These views account in large measure for the merciless criticism the book received from professional historians. France was attacked from both the right and the left for impiousness and unorthodoxy. He had expected Catholic and nationalistic reviewers to criticize him, but even historians he had considered his allies found fault with his methods, if not with his conclusions.[15]

*Immortel* or no, France was dismissed as a diletante. And it is true that he invited such conclusions. For although he was perfectly serious in *La Vie de Jeanne d'Arc,* he was possessed of enough objectivity (and irony) to consider history one of mankind's finest "amusements intellectuels."[16] From the beginning, France's serious work was balanced by comic relief. His heroine, Jeanne, was caricatured in the royalist visionary, Claudine, who appeared in the 1896 chapters of *L'Orme du mail.* The irony apparent in the second volume of the *Vie de Jeanne d'Arc* is even sharper in *L'Ile des Pingouins,* the mock history which France wrote contemporaneously with his *bona fide* work. His disappointment and anger at the *Vie*'s reception is evident in the opening pages of *L'Ile des Pingouins,* in which the following advice is given to the would-be historian:

> Les historiens se copient les uns les autres. Ils s'épargnent ainsi de la fatigue et évitent de paraître outrecuidants.

---

[15] Salomon Reinach, for example, defends France against Andrew Lang's attack but adds: "il n'est pas moin établi que M. France, admirable écrivain, historien lucide, ne sait pas ou ne sait plus travailler en érudit." (Reinach, *Cultes, Mythes et Religions,* IV, 507.)

[16] France, *La Vie littéraire II,* VI, 444.

> Imitez-les et ne soyez pas original. Un historien original est l'objet de la défiance, du mépris et du dégoût universels.[17]

France repeats his critique of historicity in *L'Ile des Pingouins:*

> Il est extrêmement difficile d'écrire l'histoire. On ne sait jamais au juste comment les choses se sont passées; et l'embarras de l'historien s'accroît avec l'abondance des documents. Quand un fait n'est connu que par un seul témoignage, on l'admet sans beaucoup d'hésitation. Les perplexités commencent lorsque les événements sont rapportés par deux ou plusieurs témoins; car leur témoignages sont toujours contradictoires et toujours inconciliables.[18]

This general observation is borne out in the analysis of the Penguin wars:

> Il est extrêmement difficile de connaître la vérité sur ces guerres, non parce que les récits manquent mais parce qu'il y en a plusieurs. Les chroniques marsouins contredisent sur tous les points les chroniques pingouins. Et, de plus, les Pingouins se contredisent entre eux, aussi bien que les Marsouins. J'ai trouvé deux chroniques qui s'accordent, mais l'un a copié l'autre.[19]

France's irony is fairly transparent in *L'Ile des Pingouins*, particularly in the contemporary episodes. His polemics are more subtle in *Les Sept Femmes de la Barbe-Bleue*, which was published the following year and serves, in effect, as an answer to his critics. The four stories in this volume not only repeat his criticism of positive action and the scientific method, but also undermine their basis in rational objectivity. This total rejection of intelligent action cannot be taken too seriously. Given a choice between science and superstition, France remains a disciple of Voltaire and Renan. But exaggeration is the prerogative of the critic.[20]

---

[17] France, *L'Ile des Pingouins, Œuvres* (Paris: Calmann-Lévy, 1929), XVIII, 5-6. Hereafter cited as *Ile*, XVIII.
[18] France, *Ile*, XVIII, 4.
[19] *Ibid.*, 139-140.
[20] Léon Blum's general observation is particularly applicable to France's attitude and technique in *Les Sept Femmes de la Barbe-Bleue:*

The mainspring of France's stories is the relationship between reality and illusion and the paradoxical values which he assigns them. Even in *La Vie de Jeanne d'Arc*, France had toyed with notions of veracity, recounting "l'histoire véridique de la fausse Jeanne d'Arc."[21] But in *Les Sept Femmes* paradox and parody, the most characteristic traits of France's thought,[22] together form the essential mechanism of the work. This paradox is not merely the tension between the real and the supernatural which is present in all fantastic tales: such non-ironic tension can be found in France's straightforward tales of mystery and suspense such as "L'Ombre" or "La Fille de Lilith."[23] In the tale of the fantastic, the supernatural intrudes into the real world, provoking undeniable and yet inexplicable events. In *Les Sept Femmes*, however, France pretends to impose the same rational evaluations on both kinds of phenomena: real and fantastic.

The longest of the stories in *Les Sept Femmes*, "La Chemise," provides a key to the others. The protagonist, Christophe V, represents the modern mentality — withering for lack of illusion. Real life is "false": we need the mysterious, the "merveilleux" which gives life its true meaning. But paradoxically, the "merveilleux" cannot exist, for if it did it would by definition annul itself.[24] France had explained the skeptic's thirst for the unknown in *La Vie littéraire:*

> Oui, nous les sages, nous aimons le merveilleux d'un amour désespéré. Nous savons qu'il n'existe pas. Nous en

---

> Or, il n'est pas de système qui soit à l'abri des circonstances et que le détail de la vie ne puisse disjoindre et recouvrir. Presque tous les systèmes sont justes quand on les affirme, et aucun ne suffit quand on l'éprouve. Mais comprenez bien qu'éprouver ce n'est pas le rôle de celui qui pense, c'est le rôle de celui qui critiquera.... Ce sont les soucis et le rôle de l'adversaire. Quand on expose l'optimisme, on écrit les *Essais de Théodicée;* quand on l'attaque, on écrit *Candide.*

(Blum, *Nouvelles Conversations de Goethe avec Eckermann, Œuvres* [Paris: Albin Michel, 1954], I, 270.)

[21] Levaillant, *Essai*, p. 654.

[22] Sareil analyzes France's style extensively in *Anatole France et Voltaire* (Genève: Droz; Paris: Minard, 1961).

[23] In *Le Livre de mon ami*, III; *Balthasar*, IV.

[24] For a more complete discussion of the relationship of the real and the supernatural in literature, see Todorov, *Introduction à la littérature fantastique* (Paris: Editions du Seuil, 1970).

sommes sûrs, et c'est même la seule chose dont nous soyons sûrs, car s'il existait il ne serait plus le merveilleux, et il n'est tel qu'à la condition de n'être pas.[25]

Christophe V's search for the magic talisman, the shirt of a happy man, is thus doomed to failure.

This paradox is incorporated into the very structure of the first three stories in the collection through France's manipulation of the traditional forms of the fairy tale and saint's legend.[26] Each of the stories is based on a "type populaire"[27] — a tale "legitimized" by a well-known text. Two, Bluebeard and the Sleeping Beauty, are taken from Perrault; the third, the legend of St. Nicolas, is based on the popular legend and children's song. These models arouse certain expectations concerning plot and character on the part of the reader, as well as fundamental concepts of reality and illusion. A simple variant or retelling of a tale may alter certain details but never changes what France has called the "fonds pueril et sacré"[28] of the story. In these irreverent versions, however, France deliberately alters these fundamental elements. The ironic tone already present in Perrault's tales is magnified in France's stories. France also exaggerates the tendency for realism which is characteristic of the French folktale (and is also emphasized in Perrault's stories).[29] France knowingly confuses this realism with historical veracity, a notion completely alien to

---

[25] France, *La Vie littéraire I*, VI, 63.
[26] Even in "La Chemise" France plays on the form of the *conte philosophique*.
[27] Georges Doutrepont, *Les Types populaires de la littérature française* (Bruxelles: Albert Dewit, 1926), I, 18. These types of characters are defined as those "consacrés par un texte littéraire qui a valeur de pièce officielle, d'extrait de naissance devant le public, même si, antérieurement, à la rédaction de ce texte, ils ont déjà circulé dans la littérature." *(Loc. cit.)*
[28] France, *La Vie littéraire IV*, VII, 459. Doutrepont elaborates on the importance of these fundamental characteristics: "Pour qu'il y ait reprise à notre sens, il faut qu'il y ait chez le remanieur le désir de refaire ou de représenter le personnage sous un aspect nouveau, mais sans que, en règle générale, la modification imposée à ce personnage le prive de son essence première ou de sa nature originelle." *(Op. cit.,* p. 337.)
[29] See e.g. Paul Delarue, *Le Conte populaire français*, I (Paris: Editions Erasme, 1957). "Ce que Perrault a fait d'un coup en simplifiant nos contes populaires, en les rendant plus raisonnables, c'est ce que le peuple fait lentement, par petites touches." (p. 43).

fiction.[30] Thus, by altering the reader's concept of fiction, he necessarily alters the perception of reality.

The satire in *Les Sept Femmes* is double. France's parodies or "reprises transformistes"[31] of traditional tales are not directed simply against his protagonists. France uses these parodies to mock scholarly and scientific methods and attitudes, much as Voltaire, in his article on Gargantua, uses the parody of a fictional character to ridicule religious beliefs. This kind of indirect attack creates an atmosphere of mock seriousness at the same time that it debases the target (by association with the fictional character). Voltaire's brief satire ends with the same paradox which France develops more extensively in his stories; what is fictional is "real," thus accepted reality must be fictional:

> Tout est impossible dans la vie de Gargantua, et c'est par cela même qu'elle est d'une vérité incontestable: car si elle n'était pas vraie, on n'aurait jamais osé l'imaginer; et la grande preuve qu'il la faut croire, c'est qu'elle est incroyable.[32]

But while Voltaire's narrator is clearly his own persona, France's satire is directed against the narrator as well as the protagonist in two of the stories, "Les Sept Femmes de la Barbe-Bleue" and "Le Grand Saint Nicolas." The events related in the stories and often the very language of the narration undermine the professed objectives of the narrator, whose unreliability is clearly revealed. In much the same way, reason founders in the face of reality in "La Chemise."

There is yet another level to France's irony in these stories. All irony (and all parody, which is inherently ironic) depends on the collaboration of *destinateur* and *destinataire* (general terms, since music and art can be parodied as well as literature); its success depends on the comprehension of indirect allusions.[33] As

---

[30] See Chapter 1 *infra*.
[31] Doutrepont, p. 352.
[32] Voltaire, *Dictionnaire philosophique III, Œuvres* (Paris: Garnier, 1879), XVIII, 215. For a complete discussion of Voltaire's influence on France see Sareil's *Anatole France et Voltaire*.
[33] For a thorough discussion of irony see e.g. Ronald Paulson, ed., *Satire: Modern Essays in Criticism* (Englewood Cliffs, N. J.: Prentice Hall, 1971).

France puts it, "Il y a, dans un beau conte, d'abord ce que l'auteur y a mis et ensuite ce que le lecteur y ajoute."[34] The reader and author form an elite which mocks the foolishness or perversity of the many. This collaboration is particularly important for France, whose style leans so heavily toward pastiche, parody and allusion. Nevertheless, France does not allow his reader to enjoy an entirely privileged position since the stories are based on the manipulation of the reader's attitudes and preconceptions. Indeed, France's technique depends on the frustration of the reader's expectations; a process which parallels the dramatic irony developed in the plot.

The humor of France's stories is Bergsonian in its contrast of the vital and the mechanical. They center on a rigid character whose expectations are constantly frustrated because he persistently fails to adapt to circumstances. France's characters are victims of illusion as well as prisoners of reality. Their rigidity is shared by narrator and reader alike, and all, to a greater or lesser degree, are implicated in France's irony. The criticism of all rational endeavor in "La Chemise" extends this irony to existential proportions, for, as Levaillant explains:

> Au lieu du triomphe possible de la raison abstraite, il évoque son échec devant l'existence, car il ne s'agit plus d'opposer des nuances d'idées, mais de montrer le contraste fondamental entre la vie vécue, les émotions éprouvées, et l'intelligence qui les comprend et ne peut rien sur elles.[35]

The pervasiveness of France's irony has been considered a form of artistic "paralysis" by some of his critics.[36] But irony is far from crippling in *Les Sept Femmes de la Barbe-Bleue*. These short stories offer a unique example of the integration of manner and form. Ironic contrast, opposition and paradox are not only used as narrative techniques but are incorporated into the basic structure of the text.

---

[34] France, *La Vie littéraire* I, VI, 123.
[35] Levaillant, *Essai*, p. 282.
[36] Such as Cerf and Chevalier.

Chapter I

"LES SEPT FEMMES DE LA BARBE-BLEUE"

The nineteenth century found Bluebeard an intriguing as well as a colorful character. The tale served as a basis for both farce and serious study. Two theatrical productions of the story were presented in Paris: *Barberouge et Barbebleue,* a vaudeville play by Dudon and Bugnoll (1852), and the better-known *opéra-bouffe Barbe-bleue* by Meilhac and Halévy, set to music by Offenbach (1866). The origins of the tale were studied by historians and cultural anthropologists. Dupuis, a pioneer of comparative religion, associated it with his general theory of sun myths; the author and ethnologist Deneulin saw a common source for the French, German and Scots versions of the story. Michelet suggested a link with the fifteenth-century nobleman Gilles de Rais. His theory was elaborated in 1855 by Eugène Bossard and popularized in 1886 by Charles Lemire.[1]

Anatole France first mentions the "Bluebeard controversy" in his "Dialogue sur les contes de fées." In a gentle spoof, he finds the blue beard, "couleur du temps" (in the best of fairytale tradition), scanty justification for an elaborate parallel with Greek and Hindu myth. Indeed, France's persona, Octave, concludes that this interpretation must be taken in the same vein as Jean-Baptiste Pérès' parody, *Le Grand Erratum,* a tenuous application of com-

---

[1] A general discussion of the origin of the Bluebeard story is found in Mary Elizabeth Storer's study, *La Mode des Contes de Fées (1685-1700),* Paris, 1928, pp. 229-230. See also P. Saintyves, *Les Contes de Perrault et les récits parallèles,* Paris, 1923.

parative mythology to the life of Napoleon which proves that the emperor was really nothing but a myth:

> ... feu mon grand'père, grand liseur de Dupuis, de Volney et de Delaure, voyait le zodiaque à l'origine de tous les cultes. Le brave homme me disait, au grand scandale de ma pauvre mère, que Jésus-Christ était le soleil, et ses douze apôtres les douze mois de l'année. Mais savez-vous, monsieur le savant, comment un homme d'esprit confondit Dupuis, Volney, Delaure et mon grand'père? Il appliqua leur théorie à l'histoire de Napoléon Ier et démontra, par ce moyen, que Napoléon n'avait pas existé, que son histoire était un mythe.... Je crains bien, Raymond, que vous ne procédiez, à l'égard de Barbe-Bleue, comme cet homme d'esprit à l'égard de Napoléon Ier.[2]

Pérès' *tour de force* consisted in proving a real figure to be a fiction. France reverses the process in "Les Sept Femmes" by treating a fictional character as if he were real. The reader should be alerted by the story's paradoxical sub-title: "d'après des documents authentiques." It is, after all, part of a collection of *contes merveilleux,* but it purports to be true. Two poles of reference, fact and fiction, are thus set in opposition: fairy tale is legitimized by factual documentation at the same time that authenticity enters the realm of fantasy. This tension is reinforced in the initial sentence:

> On a émis sur le personnage fameux, vulgairement nommé la Barbe-Bleue, les opinions les plus diverses, les plus étranges, et les plus fausses.[3]

The events described in fairy tales are often extravagant, but the concept of "true" and "false" is not a pertinent criterion in this context. The ironic use of the adverb "vulgairement" emphasizes the antithesis between a historical figure, whose fame rests on verifiable facts, and a fairy-tale character, whose basis in oral tradition epitomizes the etymological sense of the "vulgar."

---

[2] France, *Ami*, III, 414-415.

[3] France, *Les Sept Femmes de la Barbe-Bleue et autres contes merveilleux, Œuvres* (Paris: Calmann-Lévy, 1930), XIX, 127. (Hereafter cited as XIX. All further references to all stories in this volume will be given parenthetically whenever possible.)

In the "Dialogue" France showed that comparing Bluebeard to the sun was as ridiculous as comparing Napoleon to the sun. Bluebeard and Napoleon, however, were not placed on equivalent "reality scales."[4] The narrator of "Les Sept Femmes...," on the other hand, uses this comparison to expose the error of "une certaine école de mythologie comparée." He reasons that it is common knowledge that Napoleon, and (by analogy) Bluebeard, really existed: "En dépit des jeux d'esprit les plus ingénieux, on ne saurait douter que la Barbe-Bleue et Napoléon n'aient réellement existé." (128) Logic by analogy constitutes no real proof. This kind of faulty logic abounds in the story, and is one of the principal mechanisms of satirizing historical analysis.

The tension between fact and fiction is complicated by the author's ambivalent presentation of the narrator.[5] The narrator considers his "documentary evidence" to be fact, but the reader perceives it as fiction. This fiction is doubly false, however, since it contradicts the authentic version of the story, the official "biographie" handed down via Charles Perrault. The accepted facts against which the reader measures the narrator's claims are, in fact, fictional.

In an ironic way, then, Perrault merits the title of "historien" which the narrator bestows on him. However, the narrator subsequently criticizes Perrault for bias and inaccuracy: the very traits which the reader obviously sees in the narrator himself. He contends that Perrault prejudiced the public against the "real" Bluebeard in the same way that Shakespeare vilified the "real" Macbeth, again inferring by analogy that Perrault's story, like Shakespeare's play, was based on history. His long digression on the life of the historical Macbeth leads him to conclude that the real Bluebeard's life was distorted in a similar manner. France seems to have referred to the same "revue anglaise" he mentions in a similar discussion of Macbeth in *L'Histoire contemporaine*.[6] France's *alter ego*, M. Bergeret, used the example

---

[4] Cf. Todorov, *op. cit.*: "Le langage littéraire est un langage conventionnel où l'épreuve de vérité est impossible." (p. 88).

[5] It is useful to distinguish the persona of the narrator, the "Je" who is clearly trying to persuade, from an author whose language and style reveal the narrator's dishonesty.

[6] "La légende et Shakespeare, deux grandes puissances de l'esprit, en ont fait un criminel. J'ai la conviction que c'était un excellent homme. Il

of the Scottish king as a demonstration of how convincing lies can be, while the narrator in "Les Sept Femmes..." actually uses the analogy with Macbeth to mislead the reader. The comparison is further complicated by the fact that the narrator rejects the historical figure generally accepted as the prototypical French Bluebeard figure, Gilles de Rais, on the grounds that "rien dans sa vie ne ressemble à ce qu'on trouve dans celle de la Barbe-Bleue."[7] Fiction is not corrected by reality, then, but by a fictitious reality, the narrator's version of the life of Blue-Beard! History blends into poetry, and both are equally prone to distortion: "Ce ne serait pas le premier exemple d'un historien ou d'un poète qui se plaît à assombrir ses peintures." (128)

It is in this convoluted framework that the whole question of historical rehabilitation and revisionism must be considered. The historians of Gilles de Rais had claimed to "remplacer la légende par un récit authentique."[8] But their research into the life of this "triste héros"[9] resulted in a story that was even more gruesome than the fictitious accounts. Far from exonerating the maréchal, they proved that his actual crimes were much more extensive than the murder of seven wives. France's narrator also sets out to write the "véritable histoire" of an unhappy nobleman, Bernard de Montragoux, who was known popularly as Bluebeard. Unlike Gilles de Rais, however, M. de Montragoux's reputation was wholly *un*deserved — according to the narrator. Clearing the name of such a notorious scoundrel is a humorous commentary on history's ability to justify any action.

---

protégea les gens du peuple et les gens d'église contre les violences des nobles. Il fut roi économe, bon justicier, ami des artisans. La chronique l'atteste. Il n'a point assassiné le roi Duncan. Sa femme s'appelait Gruoch et avait trois vendettas contre la famille de Malcolm. Son premier mari avait été brûlé vif dans son château. J'ai là, sur ma table, dans une revue anglaise, de quoi prouver la vertu de Macbeth et l'innocence de lady Macbeth. Croyez-vous qu'en publiant ces preuves, je changerai le sentiment universel?" (France, *L'Anneau d'améthyste*, XII, 126).

[7] France, XIX, 128. The genesis for the insulting association of Bluebeard with Gilles de Rais (insulting for Bluebeard!) is found in the *Dialogue*, "...et c'est faire tort à Barbe-Bleue de le confondre avec ce terrible maréchal." (France, *Ami*, III, 413).

[8] Charles Lemire, *Un Maréchal et un connétable de France* (Paris: Ernest Leroux, 1886), p. 3.

[9] Eugène Bossard, *Gilles de Rais, Maréchal de France* (Paris: H. Champion, 1886), 2nd ed., p. XII.

But Bluebeard was not the first misunderstood victim championed by Anatole France. In light of his experience with the Dreyfus case, France's ironic question is double-edged: "Que peut la vérité froide et nue contre les prestiges étincelants du mensonge?" (130) France had had firsthand experience at combatting a generally accepted falsehood, in a situation where actions and motives were so complex that the true nature of the events remained hopelessly confused. Lies seem to have an advantage over the truth, as M. Bergeret pointed out in the *Histoire contemporaine:*

> Considérez, monsieur, que la vérité a sur le mensonge des caractères d'infériorité qui la condamnent à disparaître. D'abord elle est une, elle est une, comme dit monsieur l'abbé Lantaigne, qui l'en admire. Et vraiment il n'y a pas de quoi. Car, le mensonge étant multiple, il a contre elle le nombre. [10]

France's narrator sounds more like an attorney for the defense than an objective historian by the end of the story. He, too, presents as the truth what general opinion (as well as the author) considers falsehood. The paradox is easily resolved, however, for the reader sees through the narrator's pretense. As a more optimistic M. Bergeret had predicted of Dreyfus' accusers, the narrator is undone "par le dedans, et c'est la défaite irréparable." [11]

"From the inside" is an apt description of France's techniques in this story. The narrator is defeated by his own words. All his inferences and conclusions are faulty since his initial premise is false. This premise is also ridiculous, and the broad undercurrent of farce is essential to the story. The narrator's noble inspiration, "ce besoin de logique et de clarté qui me dévore incessamment," (129) is a parody of Rivarol's famous dictum, "Ce qui n'est pas clair n'est pas français." Clarity and precision in the realm of human events are only an illusion; the epistemological movement from intuition to "une certitude fondée sur des preuves irréfutables" is comically doomed from the start, for the unfortunate hero, for the narrator, and for mankind.

---

[10] France, *L'Anneau d'améthyste*, XII, 122.
[11] France, *M. Bergeret à Paris*, XII, 422.

One reason why Perrault's story lends itself so well to satire is the ironic tone which pervades the original version. Perrault himself played with the notion of "truthfulness" in fairy tales, and he related his stories with a mock seriousness that was obvious to his readers. All his tales are peppered with digressive comments which ostensibly demonstrate the author's candor. In fact, Perrault provides a model for an ironic rehabilitation based on first-hand, "historical" information in his "Le Petit Poucet." Lest the reader think Le Petit Poucet was too opportunistic in his harsh treatment of the ogre, Perrault supplies a magnanimous motive, verified by on-the-spot witnesses:

> Il y a bien des gens qui ne demeurent pas d'accord de cette dernière circonstance, et qui prétendent que le Petit Poucet n'a jamais fait ce vol à l'Ogre; qu'à la vérité, il n'avait pas fait conscience de lui prendre ses bottes de sept lieues, parce qu'il ne s'en servait que pour courir après les petits enfants. Ces gens-là assurent le savoir de bonne part, et même pour avoir bu et mangé dans la maison du Bûcheron. [12]

France turns the tables on Perrault, making him responsible for the errors in the account of Bluebeard's life. According to France's narrator, "il est permis de douter, sinon de sa bonne foi, du moins de la sûreté de ses informations." (128) The narrator contends that Perrault was not only misinformed but also lax in verifying his data:

> L'Historien de la Barbe-Bleue, en rapportant ces paroles, a le tort d'adopter sans contrôle la version produite, après l'événement, par les dames de Lespoisse. M. de Montagoux s'exprima tout autrement. (155)

The narrator rectifies this error by reestablishing the true words spoken by the unfortunate victim: "Les voici textuellement." (155) Such a categorical assertion is absurd. The narrator presents his own sources as impeccable: his evidence, discovered "chez

---

[12] Charles Perrault, *Contes* (Paris: Garnier Frères, 1967), 196-197. All further references to Perrault will be taken from this text and cited parenthetically whenever possible.

un tailleur de pierres de Saint-Jean-des-Bois," [13] is incontrovertible. But there is obviously no reason why we should believe this version of the story any more than the discredited version.

France's parody of historians is general, but it is likely that he had read both Bossard's and Lemire's books on Gilles de Rais because of his interest in Joan of Arc; Bossard discusses the maréchal's campaigns with Joan at length. But regardless of whether his caricature is specific or general, France succeeds completely in his imitation of scholarly tone and language. The passion for the truth expressed in the introduction of Bossard's book sounds very much like France's narrator: "L'ambition me vint donc de le faire connaître un peu plus à fond, d'après des documents originaux: je me mis en devoir de recueillir ces documents..." [14] Bossard's book is prefaced by René de Maulde, a scholar who had discovered detailed documents dealing with Gilles de Rais' trial. Unlike M. de Maulde's discovery, however, the narrator of France's story relies on "des documents authentiques" which are not altogether convincing; they amount to a diary and an anonymous denunciation. Rather than shed any real light on the subject they seem only to confirm the narrator's biases: "Ces documents me confirmèrent dans l'idée qu'il fut bon et malheureux et que sa mémoire succomba sous d'indignes calomnies." (129-30) As the story progresses, the narrator presents only that evidence which supports his theory, omitting several well-known (and incriminating) details.

France subtly undermines the authority of his narrator by allowing him to develop his thesis *ad absurdum*. His convincing arguments deteriorate rapidly. The man who is decrying a reputation based on popular opinion quotes a popular song as

---

[13] France, XIX, 129. It is not accidental that the "documents" were found at a stone quarry. Lemire points out that artifacts concerning Gilles de Rais were found in the ruins of his castle, which have become "une carrière ouverte à tous les bâtisseurs du voisinage..." (Lemire, *op. cit.*, p. 9). This authenticity is somewhat misleading, however, since the narrator's argument, like the renovations at the *château de Pierrefonds* (the scene of France's story), contains too many "pierres neuves" — new fabrications which misrepresent old truths. (See France, *Pierre Nozière*, X, 403.)

[14] Bossard, p. V. France's narrator says: "Des lors, je considérai comme un devoir d'écrire sa véritable histoire..." (XIX, 130).

evidence against Bluebeard's assassins.[15] He rejects the rumors which have spread about the fate of Bluebeard's previous wives but he accepts similar gossip to substantiate the questionable background of Bluebeard's new mother-in-law.[16] He is a master of arbitrary and false analogy. He compares the blood-stained key to Lady Macbeth's hallucinations, even though he has dismissed Shakespeare's play as a distortion of the truth; he emphasizes the horror of the plot against Bluebeard by comparing it to a similar, but completely unrelated crime — the murder "commis dans la nuit du 9 mars 1449 sur la personne de Guillaume de Flavy par Blanche d'Overbreuc, sa femme, qui était jeune et menue, le bâtard d'Orbandas, et le barbier Jean Bocquillon." (159) The precision of the names and dates of this obscure crime[17] at first appear to give the narrator an air of pompous authority; but for the average reader, the episode appears fictional with its archaic names and bizarre details. Ironically, the story is true; and Madame Blanche pleads self-defense and proves that her husband was plotting to kill her, while the wife of Bluebeard is shown to have betrayed a loving spouse!

The narrator's biases soon surface. He begins his tale in the best historical tradition, promising to reveal "la vérité froide et nue,"[18] but he quickly becomes carried away by his own rhetoric. At first he contents himself with foreshadowing the sad events to come: "Heureux s'il avait jusqu'au bout tenu son serment!"[19] Soon, however, he is speaking directly to the reader, as if he were ad-

---

[15] "Les dragons avaient la réputation de mauvais garnements, témoin la chanson: Ce sont les dragons qui viennent: / Maman, sauvons-nous!" (France, XIX, 146).

[16] See France, XIX, pp. 145, 146.

[17] France was so well-read that he had no need to invent bizarre details. The gory murder of Guillaume de Flavy was not obscure for scholars and *amateurs* of fifteenth-century history, particularly the campaigns of Joan of Arc. France could have gleaned his facts, which are quite exact — down to the "jeune et menue" — from Pierre Champion's *Guillaume de Flavy, capitaine de Compiègne; contribution à l'histoire de Jeanne d'Arc et à l'étude de la vie militaire et privée au XVème siècle* (Paris: H. Champion, 1906) or Felix Brun's *Jeanne d'Arc et le Capitaine de Soissons en 1430* (Soissons: Imprimerie de l'Argus Soissonnais, 1904).

[18] France, XIX, 130. Cf. Lemire's "récit simple et vrai" (p. 4).

[19] *Ibid.*, 143. The prophetic quality is emphasized by the disjointed syntax.

dressing a jury. The narrator is a shrewd student of courtroom technique. He implies that he is a reasonable man, willing to consider any extenuating circumstances which would explain immoral actions, by presenting an exaggerated justification:

> Le moraliste le plus austère lui trouverait des excuses, il alléguerait en faveur d'une si jeune femme les mœurs du siècle, les exemples de la ville et de la Cour, les effets trop certains d'une mère perverse.... Les sages lui pardonneraient une faute trop douce pour mériter leurs rigueurs. (157)

But these lines, written in the conditional, are indeed contrary to fact. The case in point tries the patience of even so understanding a person.

The narrator's objective presentation "d'après des documents authentiques et de sûrs témoignages" (159) quickly disintegrates into courtroom forensics, and he is not above including questionable accusations based on "certaines lettres" in his possession. Legal jargon is scattered throughout his argument: *autrement nommé, concerta, déclara, il est extrêmement probable, ce spectacle affreux, retracer, justifier, les assassins, participa au complot* (157-58). Claims of dispassionate presentation, such as, "Nous rapporterons les faits aussi sobrement que possible," (160) alternate with outbursts of emotion and extravagant epithets:

> Sa tendresse, sa bonté, son air joyeux et tranquille eussent attendri les cœurs les plus féroces. Le chevalier de la Merlus et toute cette race exécrable de Lespoisse n'y virent qu'une facilité pour attenter à sa vie.... (160)

The contrast between the professed intent and the actual delivery is obviously ironic.

The highlight of the narrator's argument reveals his limitations. This is his long digression on the nature of the famous bloodstained key. The narrator refuses to confront the "supernatural." He contends that such phenomena enter the realm of philosophy, and therefore preclude the exercise of critical judgment. This is not merely his personal opinion, but a precept supported by his venerable teacher, Monsieur Clos de Lunes, "membre de l'Institut"! [20] The *definition* of a "fairy" key is not difficult: it is a key which is "enchantée, magique, douée de propriétés contraires aux lois naturelles, telles du moins que nous les concevons." (160) The difficulty lies in determining whether or not the key was, in fact, magic. At this point the narrator has no scruples about accepting the opinions of previous historians: to wit, Perrault. He bows to the general consensus and cleverly refuses to commit himself. On the other hand, he is adamant in his contention that the key was *not* stained with blood:

> Mais où nous nous retrouvons dans notre propre domaine, ou pour mieux dire, dans notre juridiction, où nous redevenons juges des faits, arbitres des circonstances, c'est quand nous lisons que cette clef était tachée de sang. L'autorité des textes ne s'imposera pas à nous jusqu'à nous le faire croire. Elle n'était pas tachée de sang. (161)

This passage illustrates France's basic criticism of so-called objective historical methodology. The narrator's decision to accept the authorities in the first case (concerning the nature of the key) and to reject them in the second (concerning the appearance of the key) is significant. History, as represented by the narrator, does not attempt to isolate the true nature of things; it limits itself to the interpretation of appearances — and appearances can be deceiving. Moreover, all interpretations are open to reinterpretation.

Ironically, this fact works against the narrator. He is ostensibly "correcting" the error of previous historians, but his explanation of the key's red tinge is implausible, to say the least. Its unreliability is emphasized by a highly poetic, and thus conventionally fictional, language:

---

[20] This attitude is also part of the general advice given to the budding historian in *L'Ile des Pingouins:* the historian should not challenge accepted beliefs; on the contrary, he is the bastion of social institutions: "Affirmez, monsieur, que les origines de la propriété, de la noblesse, de la gendarmerie, seront traitées dans votre histoire avec tout le respect que méritent ces institutions. Faites savoir que vous admettez le surnaturel quand il se présente. A cette condition, vous réussirez dans la bonne compagnie." (France, *Ile,* XVIII, 6).

ce que, dans son trouble, *l'épouse criminelle* prit sur *l'acier* pour une tache de sang était un reflet du ciel encore tout *empourpré* des *roses de l'aurore*. (162; italics mine)

The impossibility of establishing objective truth is, then, an underlying theme of the story. Two opposing processes are in play: Bluebeard's rehabilitation (the correction of a supposed misconception), and the simultaneous discrediting of that correction. The implications are clear: the stories told by historians are as treacherous as fiction.

The basic stylistic mechanism at work in "Les Sept Femmes de la Barbe-Bleue" can be compared to the *cliché renouvelé*. A well-known pattern has been altered, and a momentary shock is caused by the implicit contrast between what is expected and what in fact occurs. This effect is intensified by the many references to Perrault's story which provide a series of explicit contrasts and serve as the basis for the narrator's rehabilitation of Bluebeard. The story's impact would be lost on a reader unfamiliar with the original fairy tale.[21] As in all parody, the humor (and irony) lies largely outside the text in the realm of comparison; the interface or *intertextualité* which exists in the reader's mind.

In addition, France overlaps *forme* and *fond,* and makes frustrated expectations a central theme of the story as well as a stylistic device. The assumptions of both the reader and the hero are unfulfilled — with one important difference. The reader has been "let in" on the joke: France uses irony, parody, and other stylistic markers to undermine the story presented by the narrator, and thus reinforces the reader's preconceptions after having provoked an initial reaction of surprise. In contrast, the delusions of the unfortunate M. de Montragoux are used to demonstrate that man learns nothing from experience, or, by extension, from History.

---

[21] Sareil has analyzed a similar use of this technique in France's story "Le Procurateur de Judée" (*Romanic Review*, LXI, No. 4 [Dec. 1970], 287-295). He points out that the irony in that story is essentially humorless; an elaborate preparation for the final punch line. But "Les Sept Femmes..." is a longer and more complex story, and this difference is reflected in its technique.

The goal of historical rehabilitation is to change a widely-held opinion. France's narrator therefore tells the story of Bluebeard in a way which will present the facts in a new light and presumably convince the reader that he has misjudged this notorious personage. The reader's basic attitudes concerning the Bluebeard story can be divided into two main categories: definite notions about the personalities of the characters and certain expectations of the fairy-tale structure in which their adventures are related. The sequence and nature of the actions are predetermined, and any deviations are perceived immediately. Moreover, the rigid and nearly abstract form of fairy tales is hostile to extraneous detail; the few characteristics and objects which are specified are generally highly symbolic.[22] History, in contrast, abounds in details. One of the aims of historians is the arranging and interpretation of seemingly haphazard facts. In his effort to convince us that his story is historical, then, the narrator deluges us with supporting details, using techniques of addition, justification, and (because he is not the most scrupulous scholar) omission.

Bluebeard's rehabilitation may have been inspired by Perrault's version of the tale. The *second* moral of the 17th century story indicates that even the fiercest husbands are a hen-pecked lot:

> Il n'est plus d'époux si terrible,
> Ni qui demande l'impossible,
> Fût-il malcontent et jaloux.
> Près de sa femme on le voit filer doux;
> Et de quelque couleur que sa barbe puisse être,
> On a peine à juger qui des deux est le maître. (129)

Perrault also gives broad hints that Bluebeard's last wife, if not an outright adventuress, is at least far from guiltless. She marries Bluebeard for his money; after seeing his extensive possessions she decides "que les Maître du logis n'avait plus la barbe si bleue, et que c'était un fort honnête homme." (123) Her cupidity is even

---

[22] Max Lüthi discusses fairy-tale structure in his *Once Upon a Time: On the nature of fairy tales* (New York: Frederick Ungar, 1970). A more detailed discussion of structure can be found in Vladimir Propp's classic, *La Morphologie du conte* (Paris: Editions du Seuil, 1965); much of his discussion of folk tales is applicable to written fairy tales as well as the oral tradition: see Chapter V *infra*.

more obvious when she abandons her guests (a serious breach of etiquette in the seventeenth century) and recklessly rushes to see what treasures are contained in the forbidden room "avec tant de précipitation qu'elle pensa se rompre le cou *deux ou trois fois*." [23] Finally, when her disobedience is discovered, she throws herself on her husband's mercy — not truly repentant but "avec toutes les marques d'un vrai repentir." (126)

Nevertheless, Perrault's Bluebeard remains a villain, albeit a gentleman. He is introduced in traditionally succinct terms: "Il était une fois un homme qui avait de belles maisons à la Ville et à la Campagne, de la vaisselle d'or et d'argent, des meubles en broderie, et des carrosses tout dorés; mais par malheur cet homme avait la Barbe bleue." (123) In contrast, the first words of France's narrator show us we are dealing with an altogether different story. Gone is the "once upon a time." This is History: names, dates and locations:

> Vers 1650 résidait sur ses terres entre Campiègne et Pierrefonds, un riche gentilhomme, nommé Bernard de Montragoux, dont les ancêtres avaient occupé les plus grandes charges du royaume; (131)

These details are by no means arbitrary. First, they preclude any possible association with the historical Bluebeard, Gilles de Rais, who lived in Brittany in the early 15th century. Since Perrault's story provides the "historical" basis for France's narrator, the action takes place just prior to the first publication of Perrault's *Contes de ma Mère l'oye*.[24] These details also add local color and an air of authenticity. Monsieur de Montragoux's castle, "bâti aux temps gothiques," is located near the site of Viollet-le-Duc's renovation of a feudal castle. In addition, the description of the castle furnishes an interesting correlative to its owner's personality. Like Bernard de Montragoux, Les Guillettes seems austere and forboding, but its outward appearance is misleading:

> Il se montrait de dehors assez farouche et morose, avec les tronçons de ses grosses tours abattues lors des trou-

---

[23] Perrault, 124. Italics mine.
[24] In 1695.

> bles du royaume, au temps du feu roi Louis. Au-dedans
> il offrait un aspect plus agréable. (132)

The narrator attempts to legitimize his hero's appearance through a series of comparisons in which his unique beard is reduced to a mere five o'clock shadow. These comparisons elucidate the narrator's train of thought. Bluebeard is not mythical but real: thus he is first compared negatively to a Greek god, then, also negatively, to a series of fictitious but historically situated "ancestors," and finally, positively, to a real person:

> Il ne faut pas se représenter M. de Montragoux sous l'aspect monstrueux du triple Typhon qu'on voit à Athènes, riant dans sa triple barbe indigo. Nous nous approcherons bien davantage de la réalité en comparant le seigneur des Guillettes à ces comédiens ou à ces prêtres dont les joues fraîchement rasées ont des reflets d'azur. M. de Montragoux ne portait pas sa barbe en pointe comme son grand-père à la Cour du roi Henri II; il ne la portait pas en éventail comme son bisaïeul, qui fut tué à la bataille de Marignan. Ainsi que M. de Turenne, il n'avait qu'un peu de moustache et la mouche. (133)

This argument might be convincing had not the reader been previously put on guard by the disturbing coda attached to the narrator's initial attempt at explaining M. de Montragoux's appearance: "Ses joues paraissaient bleues; mais quoi qu'on ait dit, ce bon seigneur n'en était point défiguré, et ne faisait point peur *pour cela*." (133; italics mine)

The familiar tale of Bluebeard's violence and cunning is prefaced by a saga of six unhappy marriages, in which the husband is always the injured party. This new Bluebeard is characterized by generosity, tenderness, naïveté, and of course, timidity, the source of all his problems. His erratic behavior is an outlet for emotional stress; his rumored cruelty is founded on one or two slaps dealt in exasperation to his fifth wife whose indiscretions were obvious even to the gullible M. de Montragoux.[25]

---

[25] This marriage is a parody of Mme. de Lafayette's seventeenth-century novel, *La Princesse de Clèves*. The novel's innocent villain, M. de Clèves, is the victim of his own noble sentiments. He assures his wife she can

One of the story's basic ironies is the perception shared by the author and reader of the hero's incredulity. Bluebeard is presented as a completely ingenuous (and neurotic) character. The traditional innocent, for example, Voltaire's famous *ingénu,* is disquietingly perceptive; his candor permits frank social criticism. Bluebeard, on the contrary, is truly simple. He is not even sure what he is suspicious of: "La pauvre Barbe-Bleue se doutait bien de quelque chose, mais il ne savait pas de quoi." (139)

Bluebeard is introduced to the reader as the victim of a classic approach-avoidance syndrome. He is paralyzed by his emotions, which are expressed by a series of antitheses:

> Les dames exerçaient sur lui un invincible *attrait* et lui faisaient une *peur* insurmontable. Il les *craignait* autant qu'il les *aimait.* (134; italics mine)

His choice of a new wife is characterized by a similar antithesis: "Ayant été trompé par une femme d'esprit, une sotte le rassurait." (140) This aphoristic commentary is a striking illustration of Bluebeard's emotional tension. After five marriages he has learned nothing, and the sight of a pretty woman still arouses violent and contradictory emotions in him: "Il suffisait de la vue de mademoiselle de Pontalcin pour réveiller à la fois ses tourments et ses forces." (142) Even his jealousy is characterized by the same kind of stalemate:

---

confide in him and suffers the consequences. The princess stresses her innocence in her confession:

> Eh bien, monsieur, lui répondit-elle en se jetant à ses genoux, je vais vous faire un aveu que l'on n'a jamais fait à son mari, mais l'innocence de ma conduite et de mes intentions m'en donne la force. (Mme. de Lafayette, *La Princesse de Clèves,* New York: Charles Scribner's Sons, 1930), p. 112.

This innocence is caricatured in the simple-minded candor of Angèle, Bluebeard's fifth spouse:

> Angèle était bien trop candide pour lui rien cacher. Elle lui disait: 'Monsieur, on m'a dit ceci; on m'a fait ceci; on m'a pris ceci; j'ai vu cela; j'ai senti cela.' Et, par son ingénuité, elle faisait souffrir à ce pauvre seigneur des tourments inimaginables. (France, XIX, 141)

The parody is reinforced by a second parallel with Mme. de Lafayette, see p. 36, *infra,* note 26.

> La pauvre Barbe-Bleue, apprenant d'un seul coup son abondant déshonneur et la fin tragique de sa femme, ne se consola pas de ce second malheur en considération du premier.[26]

The ultimate reflection of Bluebeard's paradoxical emotional life can be seen in his unflagging optimism and constant frustration. His expectations are always disappointed:

> Il épousa Mademoiselle de la Garandine et s'aperçut de la fausseté de ses prévisions. (140)

> La Barbe-Bleue, qui se promettait de goûter entre ses bras un bonheur infini, fut une fois de plus trompé dans ses espérances.... (142)

But this picture of Bluebeard's innocence is ironic. We are amused and at the same time unconvinced. Even a naïve reader would grow suspicious of Monsieur de Montragoux. If his nickname is undeserved, his Christian name is no more reassuring. His failures in no way diminish his desires, and the narrator seems at a loss to account for his hero's continued amorous adventures. There are only two logical explanations: Bluebeard is either a sexual maniac or too stupid to learn from experience. The lame excuses offered by the narrator lead us to believe that both possibilities are likely. Monsieur de Montragoux's insatiable appetites are brushed aside with an obvious and unsatisfactory cliché:

---

[26] France, XIX, 140. This scene is another echo of *La Princesse de Clèves:* the prince's *récit* of Sancerre and Mme. de Tournon. France's succinct phrasing is a humorous condensation of the lengthy emotional torment described by Mme. de Lafayette:

> Je serais trop heureux de l'avoir perdue, et la vie, s'écria-t-il. Madame de Tournon m'était infidèle, et j'apprends son infidélité et sa trahison le lendemain que j'ai appris sa mort, dans un temps où mon âme est remplie et pénétrée de la plus vive douleur et de la plus tendre amour que l'on ait jamais sentie.... Je trouve que je me suis trompé, qu'elle ne mérite pas que je la pleure; cependant j'ai la même affliction de sa mort que si elle m'était fidèle, et je sens son infidélité comme si elle n'était point morte. Si j'avais appris son changement devant sa mort, la jalousie, la colère, la rage m'auroient rempli, et m'auroient endurci en quelque sorte contre la douleur de sa perte; mais je suis dans un état où je ne puis ni m'en consoler ni la haïr.

(*La Princesse de Clèves*, p. 56.)

> Après une si funeste expérience, comment la Barbe-Bleue se résolut-il à contracter une nouvelle union? C'est ce qu'on ne pouvait comprendre si l'on ne savait le pouvoir d'un bel œil sur un cœur bien né. (141)

And after recounting the tale of six disastrous marriages, the narrator has the effrontery to claim that his hero's innocence is due to lack of experience: "Son expérience des femmes ne suffisait pas à le rendre soupçonneux, et il ne se défiait pas de ce qu'il aimait." (149)

This slightly tarnished hero becomes the prey of professional fortune-hunters. Bluebeard's newly acquired innocence is more than balanced by the villany of his seventh wife's relatives, the Lespoisse family. France elaborates at length on the details given in Perrault's story. Perrault's single sentence of introduction: "Une de ses voisines, dame de qualité, avait deux filles parfaitement belles," (123) is amended with ample and derogatory epithets. The "dame de qualité" becomes a "veuve sur le retour," (145) and the perfect beauty of her daughters is belied by the fact that "L'aînée, Anne, près de coiffer St. Catherine, était une fine mouche. Jeanne, la plus jeune, bonne à marier, cachait sous les apparences de l'ingénuité une précoce expérience du monde." (146) Thus the girls' beauty, like Bluebeard's ferocious appearance, is deceiving. France makes the point even more explicitly: "Jeanne la cadette... était plus fraîche, ce qui ne veut pas dire qu'elle était plus neuve." (148) The two brothers in the family remain "l'un Dragon et l'autre Mousquetaire" as the were in Perrault's story. But they are no longer introduced at the last minute as heroes. Their bad character is established at the outset. Here again, appearances are inconclusive. Pierre de Lespoisse is a black musketeer, but his rank "n'y paraissait pas quand il allait à pied." (146) (After giving this disturbing detail France adds that musketeers were distinguished by the color of their horse's accoutrements rather than by their uniforms.)

The pretense and *faux brillant* of the entire family can be seen in the description of Bluebeard's marriage to Jeanne. France accumulates elegant and dignified details: *la demoiselle Jeanne, madame leur mère, le chevalier de la Merlus, une magnificence extraordinaire, une beauté suprenante, un éclat sans pareil.* (151)

But this impression of elegance and nobility is immediately destroyed by a single sentence which contrasts both in style and content with the preceding description:

> Sitôt après la cérémonie, les juifs, qui avaient loué à la famille et au greluchon de la mariée ces belles nippes et ces riches joyaux, les reprirent et les emportèrent en poste à Paris. (151)

Of course, Monsieur de Montragoux is included in this show of respectability, and it would not be exaggerating to infer that he, too, was putting on a false front.

In a similar way, the sarcasm which is often used to disparage Bluebeard's antagonists undermines his own character descriptions as well. When Bluebeard's scheming mother-in-law is called "honnête," her sons' vile tricks "bon tours," and a reprobate monk "ce bon religieux," the epithets are clearly sarcastic. But if this technique is consistent throughout the story, the many qualifications of Bluebeard as "bon" or "pauvre" must also be ironic. Of course, authors are not obliged to be consistent; but in this case, the narrator is supposed to be presenting a coherent and logical argument. The narrator has been written into a bind, and the premise of Bluebeard's innocence is seriously eroded.

This revised cast of characters figures in the retelling of Perrault's story. The original text is a standard; hence there are many instances of paraphrasing or direct quotation. For example, compare the following passages:

| France | Perrault |
|---|---|
| Il se rendit en grand équipage à la Motte Giron et fit sa demande à la dame de Lespoisse, lui laissant le choix de celle de ses filles qu'elle voudrait lui donner. (147) | Il lui en demanda une en mariage, et lui laissa le choix de celle qu'elle voudrait lui donner. (123) |
| Faites venir vos bonnes amies, madame, lui dit-il, et les menez promener; divertissez-vous et faites bonne chère. (154) | il la priait de se bien divertir pendant son absence, qu'elle fît venir ses bonnes amies, qu'elle les menât à la campagne si elle voulait, que partout elle fît bonne chère. (124) |

Most of the time, however, the references to Perrault have been either significantly altered or amended, so that they simultaneously recall the original and contrast with it. For example, France's text is definitely more lascivious in the following example:

| France | Perrault |
|---|---|
| Sa jeune épouse l'accueillit d'un air souriant, se laissa accoler et conduire dans la chambre conjugale, et fit tout au gré de l'excellent homme. (160) | Sa femme fit tout ce qu'elle put pour lui témoigner qu'elle était ravie de son prompt retour. (126) |

Perrault's text often furnishes the starting point for elaborate justifications and detailed additions. The narrator manipulates his sources carefully. For example, he first quotes Perrault for authority, but casts doubt on his accuracy:

> Charles Perrault dit qu'un mois après avoir contracté cette union la Barbe-Bleue fut obligée de faire un voyage de six semaines pour une affaire de conséquence; mais il semble ignorer les motifs de ce voyage...[27]

Shortly thereafter he quotes Perrault at length (so that the source is unmistakable) but stops short of a key passage, the famous interdiction:

> Voilà, lui dit-il, les clefs des deux grandes garde-meubles; voilà celle de la vaisselle d'or et d'argent, qui ne sert pas tous les jours; voilà celle de mes coffres-forts, où est mon or et mon argent; celles de mes cassettes où sont mes pierreries, et voilà le passe-partout de tous les appartements. Pour cette petite clef-là, c'est la clef du cabinet, au bout de la grande galerie de l'appartement bas; ouvrez-tout, allez partout. (154)

Bluebeard's prohibition is conspicuously absent. Once this discrepancy has registered with the reader, however, the missing sentence is supplied, but only as a negative reference:

---

[27] France, XIX, 154. Cf. Perrault: "Au bout d'un mois la Barbe-bleue dit à sa femme qu'il était obligé de faire un voyage en Province, de six semaines au moins, pour une affaire de conséquence." (p. 123). It is worth noting that Perrault's Bluebeard only *says* he has a business trip.

> Charles Perrault prétend que M. de Montragoux ajouta: Mais pour ce petit cabinet, je vous défends d'y entrer, et je vous le défends de telle sorte que, s'il vous arrive de l'ouvrir, il n'y a rien que vous ne deviez attendre de ma colère. (154-55)

Still another contrast is created when M. de Montragoux's "true" statement, an overly solicitous appeal to his wife, follows Perrault's discredited but still striking warning:

> Vous pouvez donc entrer dans ce petit cabinet comme dans toutes les autres chambres de ce logis; mais, si vous m'en croyez, vous n'en ferez rien, pour m'obliger et en considération des idées douloureuses que j'y attache et des mauvais présages que ces idées font naître malgré moi dans mon esprit. Je serais désolé qu'il vous arrivât malheur... (155-56)

The impact of Perrault's interdiction depends on the mysterious quality of the *petit cabinet*. But France has defused this effect by introducing an explanation of the room's unhappy connotations for Monsieur de Montragoux early in the story. Again, he quotes Perrault for authority but amends his remarks:

> A l'une des extrémités de cette galerie se trouvait un cabinet qu'on appelait ordinairement 'le petit cabinet.' C'est le seul nom dont Charles Perrault le désigne. Il n'est pas inutile de savoir qu'on le nommait aussi le cabinet des princesses infortunées, parce qu'un peintre de Florence avait représenté sur les murs les tragiques histoires de Dircé, fille du Soleil..., de Niobé... de Procris...[28]

On the other hand, when Perrault's text corroborates his own thesis, France's narrator is only too glad to quote him accurately. Nevertheless, the authority of the quoted text is often used as an umbrella for his own, biased additions. For example, he af-

---

[28] France, XIX, 132. This detail may have been suggested by the frescoes of the chapel of Saint Nicolas, which were discovered in the 18th century and played an important role in the controversy over the source of the Bluebeard legend. They ostensibly portray the life of Saint Triphine, but graphically illustrate Perrault's tale. Bossard and Deulin are convinced that the written story influenced the painter, and not vice versa.

firms Perrault's description of the wife's impatience to enter the *petit cabinet,* but adds an ulterior motive:

> ... comme l'a dit Perrault, 'elle fut si pressée de sa curiosité que, sans considérer qu'il était malhonnête de quitter sa compagnie, elle y descendit par un petit escalier dérobé, et avec tant de précipitation qu'elle pensa se rompre le cou deux ou trois fois.' Le fait n'est pas douteux. Mais ce que personne n'a dit, c'est qu'elle n'était si impatiente de pénétrer en ce lieu que parce que le chevalier de la Merlus l'y attendait. (156)

Perrault's text is often significantly altered in order to enhance Bluebeard's good qualities or to cast aspersions on his antagonists. For instance, the following reference is a direct quote from Perrault, but the narrator suggests that it is backed by a host of authorities:

> Tous les historiens qui ont traité ce sujet ajoutent que Madame de Montragoux ne se divertissait pas à voir toutes ces richesses, à cause de l'impatience qu'elle avait d'aller ouvrir le petit cabinet. (156)

The alterations to Perrault's text are not always obvious. Compare the following passages:

| France | Perrault |
|---|---|
| Pour faire connaissance, la Barbe-Bleue invita Anne et Jeanne de Lespoisse avec leur mère, leurs frères et une multitude de dames et de gentilshommes, à passer quinze jours au château des Guillettes. (146) | La Barbe-bleue, pour faire connaissance, les mena avec leur mère, et trois ou quatre de leurs meilleures amies, et quelques jeunes gens du voisinage, à une de ses maisons de Campagne, où on demeura huit jours entiers. (123) |

Perrault's text has been changed only to emphasize Bluebeard's largesse: the number of guests and the length of the festivities have been increased. Having stretched the truth a little, the narrator goes on to add a detailed description of the host's "rare magnificence," and then authenticates his extrapolation by referring back to Perrault directly:

> On ne dormait point pendant ces merveilleuses réjouissances et, comme le dit l'auteur de la plus ancienne histoire de la Barbe-Bleue, 'l'on passait toute la nuit à se faire des malices les uns aux autres.' (150)

But this quotation is in turn expanded with an account of the evening's ribald amusements, which illustrate Bluebeard's endless patience (and stupidity) and his guests' bad faith.

Perrault's text is not only amended and explicated, it is strategically abridged as well. The concluding sentence is a good example. France eliminates the derogatory reference to Bluebeard and at the same time gives an ironic twist to the personality of his wife's new husband — no stranger in this case:

| FRANCE | PERRAULT |
|---|---|
| La Barbe-Bleue n'avait point d'héritiers. Sa veuve demeura maîtresse de ses biens. Elle en employa une partie à doter sa sœur Anne, une autre partie à acheter des charges de capitaines à ses deux frères, et le reste à se marier elle-même avec le chevalier de la Merlus, qui devint un très honnête homme dès qu'il fut riche. (163) | Il se trouva que la Barbe-bleue n'avait point d'héritiers, et qu'ainsi sa femme demeura maîtresse de tous ses biens. Elle en employa une partie à marier sa sœur Anne avec une jeune gentilhomme, dont elle était aimée depuis longtemps, une autre partie à acheter des charges de capitaine à ses deux frères; et le reste à se marier elle-même à un fort honnête homme, qui lui fit oublier les mauvais temps qu'elle avait passés avec la Barbe-bleue. (128) |

France's narrator is just as quick to eliminate details which work against his purpose as he is to supply motivations when Bluebeard's actions seemed suspicious. He keeps only those details which stress Bluebeard's warmth and generosity, and does not indicate his deletions. For example:

> 'Les voisines et les bonnes amies,' dit Charles Perrault, 'n'attendirent pas qu'on les envoyât quérir pour aller chez la jeune mariée, tant elles avaient d'impatience de voir toutes les richesses de sa maison.' (156)

France stops here, but Perrault continues, "n'ayant osé y venir pendant que le Mari y était, à cause de sa Barbe bleue qui leur faisait peur." (124)

Another incriminating detail is the date of Bluebeard's return. Perrault states that it was "dès le soir même." Since the unexpected return is an essential element of the story, it cannot be eliminated. France's narrator therefore skirts the issue by simply stating that "La Barbe-Bleue revint un peu plus tôt qu'on ne l'attendait," (160) — but his understatement is ironic for any reader familiar with the original story. The statement is so weak that the narrator immediately takes the offensive and denies any motive of jealousy on the part of M. de Montragoux — thereby firmly establishing that motive in the mind of the reader:

> C'est ce qui a fait croire bien faussement que, en proie aux soupçons d'une noire jalousie, il voulait surprendre sa femme. Joyeux et confiant, s'il pensait lui faire une surprise, c'était une surprise agréable. (160)

The narrator's interpretation of Bluebeard's motive has completely reversed the traditional plot. Similar reversals of situation or character traits are used elsewhere for humorous effect. The surrender of the infamous blood-stained key is one of the high points of Perrault's story: the suspicious husband demands the missing key, notices the tell-tale spot, and threatens the life of his disobedient wife. In contrast, France's hero asks for the key "doucement." He finds that it is not crusted with blood; on the contrary:

> Il observa, en effet, que cette clef apparaissait maintenant plus nette et plus brillante que lorsqu'il l'avait donnée, et pensa que ce poli ne pouvait venir que de l'usage. (162)

The effect remains the same in both stories — the wife's disobedience is discovered — but the cause has been reversed. France juggles the reactions to this disobedience as well. Instead of the furor expected by the reader, Bluebeard reacts with exaggerated sensibility. "Sa tendresse, sa bonté, son air joyeux eussent attendri les cœurs les plus féroces." (160) This is a direct reversal of Perrault's version, where Bluebeard's distraught wife "aurait attendri un rocher... mais la Barbe-bleue avait le cœur plus dur qu'un rocher." (126) And in a climactic tour de force, France transforms Bluebeard's threat into a sigh of regret: "Si vous y demeuriez soumise à votre tour, je ne m'en consolerais pas." (162)

France combines this technique (anticipating and contradicting the reader's expectations) with the theme of thwarted expectations in the conclusion of the story. The brevity and quick pace of the closing lines make the final series of misunderstandings even more striking — and more humorous. It is worth while to examine these lines in detail. First, it is Bluebeard's turn for surprise. His lament is met by hysterical screams despite his reasonable expectations, indicated by the conjunctions *bien que* and *car:*

> A ces mots, bien que la Barbe-Bleue ne pût lui faire peur, car son langage et son maintien n'exprimaient que la mélancolie et l'amour, la jeune dame de Montragoux se mit à crier à tue-tête: —Au secours! On me tue! (162)

(The irony of this reaction is that it is what one would expect if Bluebeard were "really" behaving like Bluebeard.) Next, his wife is deceived when her murder plot does not work as planned:

> C'était le signal convenu. En l'entendant le chevalier de la Merlus et les deux fils de Madame de Lespoisse devaient se jeter sur la Barbe-Bleue et le percer de leurs épées. Mais le chevalier, que Jeanne avait caché dans une armoire de la chambre, parut seul. (162)

The reader is next in turn for disappointment, for the tower scene with its famous line: "Anne, ma sœur Anne, ne vois-tu rien venir?" (126) has been conspicuously eliminated:

> Jeanne s'enfuit, épouvantée, et rencontra dans la galerie sa sœur Anne, qui n'était pas, comme on l'a dit, sur une tour, car les tours du château avaient été abattues par l'ordre du cardinal de Richelieu. (162)

The allusion to the missing scene makes its absence even more noticeable, and a final contrast is added by the historical detail which clashes with the (absent) fairy-tale context.

France maintains the suspense of the original story concerning the arrival of the wife's brothers, but he has reversed the nature of this suspense. "Sœur Anne" hastens her brothers on in both stories — but unlike Perrault's heroes, France's brothers are cowards "qui, pâles et chancelants, n'osaient risquer un si grand coup." As a final sign of their ignominy, the brothers stab Bluebeard in the back and "le frappèrent encore longtemps après qu'il eut expiré." (163)

The contrasts with Perrault's story, both explicit and implicit, are the most striking features of "Les Sept Femmes de la Barbe-Bleue." But France's continuous undercutting of Bluebeard's rehabilitation is furthered by many less obvious stylistic devices. The cumulative effect of the digressive, ironic, and licentious remarks scattered throughout the story goes far to demolish the narrator's argument. On close inspection, his seemingly elegant and logical construction proves to be a crumbling facade.

Beneath the surface of factual presentation, for example, there are traces of fairy-tale narrative. Hearsay and speculation are common devices used in folktales for heightening suspense; France uses these techniques to discuss Mme. de Lespoisse's origins and the fate of Bluebeard's wives.[29] Elements of fairy tales are parodied in the episode involving Bluebeard's fifth wife, Angèle de la Garandine. In addition to her childish ingenuousness à la Mme. de Clèves, she is gullible enough to believe she will meet the archangel Gabriel in the woods. France mocks her simple-minded faith by adding a touch of cupidity; she is tempted to make a rendez-vous by the promise of pearl garters. Appropriately, the beginning and end of this episode are parodies of fairy-tale situations:

> Les médecins, ayant employé divers médicaments sans effet, l'avertirent que le seul remède convenable à son mal était de prendre une jeune épouse.[30]

> On croit que le loup la mangea, car on ne la revit onques plus. (141)

A sick king who can be cured only by a miraculous remedy is a common opening plot (cf. *La Chemise*). Often this situation pro-

---

[29] France, XIX, 145, 146. Cf. Perrault, p. 101 *(La Belle au Bois dormant)*.
[30] *Ibid.*, 140. Cf. Propp's index of *situations initiales*.

vides the specification of the task which the hero must accomplish; or, a love-sick hero may have seen the portrait of an unknown beauty and set off to find her. An unnatural attachment of an old king for a young princess is the opening situation of Perrault's *Peau d'Ane*. However, when the protagonist is Bluebeard and the specific remedy is a fifth young wife, no speculation on the nature of the illness is necessary. As for the conclusion of the episode, it is the classic punishment of wicked children, and the archaic *oncques* emphasizes its roots in oral tradition.

Even when the narrator's information is completely factual, it sometimes has the opposite of the desired effect. The task of the historian is to sort out details and discard irrelevant facts, thereby arriving at some general truth. France's narrator substantiates his argument with totally pointless and often disconcerting details. For example, Bluebeard's fourth wife, Blanche de Gibeaumex, is the daughter of an "officier de cavalerie qui n'avait qu'une oreille; il disait avoir perdu l'autre au service du roi." (139) Did her father lose his ear honorably or not? And what does it matter? This is overkill with facts.

The use of irony — saying one thing and meaning another — is the most natural technique for belying the story presented by the narrator. France uses irony in different ways, however. The narrator, as we have seen, makes ironic remarks to denigrate Bluebeard's antagonists. His implications are made perfectly clear, often by the use of syntactical devices or antitheses and oxymorons too blatant to be overlooked:

> Il fit sa demande, que Madame de Lespoisse agréa, bien que son cœur se déchirât, *disait-elle,* à la pensée de marier ses filles. (151)

> ...*madame sa mère, la plus adroite coquine* de tout le royaume de France... (153)

> Son frère était, auprès de lui, un *honnête garçon. Ivrogne et joueur*.... (147)

> Le chevalier de la Merlus *se perdait de préférence* avec Jeanne de Lespoisse. (148; all italics mine)

But ironic contrasts also work against the narrator. The juxtaposition of incongruous ideas often causes the reader to reevaluate the facts. This technique is perfectly suited to the basic theme of the story: a questioning of the whole process of rational interpretation.

Monsieur de Montragoux is "unrehabilitated" by a series of such contrasts. The depth of his attachment for his first wife seems doubtful, considering that he "la pleurait encore quand il lui advint de danser, à la fête des Guillettes, avec Jeanne de la Cloche." (137) A similar effect is created after his second wife's demise when the declaration of his grief is followed by a rapid remarriage:

> Chose difficile à croire, et pourtant certaine, son époux fut affligé de cette mort, tant il avait l'âme pittoyable.
> Six semaines après l'accident il épousa sans cérémonie Gigonne, la fille de son fermier Tragnel. (138)

The separation of these two actions by the start of a new paragraph emphasizes the abruptness of his change of heart.

The elements of the ironic contrast are not always juxtaposed so prominently, but they are no less present. For example:

> Il faisait sa cour à cette jeune demoiselle le mieux qu'il pouvait, lui parlant peu, faute d'habitude, mais il la regardait en roulant des yeux terribles et en tirant du fond des entrailles des soupirs à renverser un chêne. (148)

The discrepancy between a *demoiselle* and a *chêne,* between *faisait sa cour* and *en roulant des yeux terribles* is unsettling, as is the implicit contrast between the traditional, metaphorical heart and M. de Montragoux's lovesick *entrailles.* As is often the case, the irony here is double. We can see yet another example of the unfortunate mismatching of Bluebeard's intentions and the results; or we can see a demented Don Juan in the place of a lovesick hero.

Another delayed effect is created by the string of comparatives which considerably lessens the intensity of Bluebeard's "unique" passion for his fourth wife:

> Il aimait Blanche de Gibeaumex d'une ardeur singulière et plus chèrement qu'il n'avait aimé Jeanne de la Cloche, Gigonne Traignel, et même Colette Passage. (140)

Other ironic contrasts call into question the narrator's powers of judgment rather than directly casting suspicion on Bluebeard. When the narrator completely misconstrues a fact which is obvious to the reader, how can he be trusted? The narrator's interpretation of Bluebeard's behavior in the presence of a woman is a good example. Whenever M. de Montragoux saw a woman, "ses sentiments ne se faisaient jour que par ses yeux, qu'ils roulaient d'une manière effroyable. Cette timidité..." (134) Timidity is hardly the explanation for Bluebeard's reaction, and the narrator's conclusion is made even more striking by the close juxtaposition of *effroyable* and *timidité*.

Even the alibi for Bluebeard's sudden business trip is retroactively discredited by a bizarre detail:

> M. de Montragoux se rendit dans le Perche pour recueillir l'héritage de son cousin d'Outarde, tué glorieusement d'un boulet de canon à la bataille des Dunes, tandis qu'il jouait aux dés sur un tambour. (154)

Monsieur d'Outarde's glory is quickly dimmed by his inglorious pastime, and the whole digressive anecdote strikes a note of humor in the midst of a "serious" explanation.

The close relationship of irony and the art of false logic in France's work has been discussed by Levaillant.[31] Distorted logic permeates "Les Sept Femmes..." on every level. France often sets up an elaborately symmetrical structure only to contrast it with a syllepsis such as "vomissant l'injure et le vin" (137) or "il était maître de lui-même comme des Guillettes." (143) Physical and spiritual qualities are contrasted in the falsely symmetrical description, "un mari d'une si haute condition et d'une si forte corpulence." (134) This discrepancy is reinforced by the true parallels which precede and follow it: "Il l'aimait de tout son pouvoir et de toutes ses forces" and "le plus obéissant des serviteurs et le plus épris des amants." Still another contrast between literal and figurative meaning can be seen in this pair of prepositional phrases: "Elle le trompait dans son château et jusque sous ses yeux sans qu'il s'en aperçut." (139)

---

[31] With regard to *Thaïs*. See Levaillant, p. 275 ff.

At the same time that he plays havoc with rational logic, France sets up a subliminal system of relationships which are absurdly logical. Bluebeard's first wife is the trainer of a dancing bear; she runs off with the bear and M. de Montragoux, the gruff, lumbering hero, meets Number 2 while dancing. Bluebeard puts catnip in his second wife's wine in order to cure her alcoholism, but catlike, she "bondit sur lui" (138) and inflicts a serious wound. The third wife, who "sentait l'oignon" (138) dies in a very plantlike way: "Elle sécha de dépit, et en prit une jaunisse dont elle mourut." (139) And finally, while Bluebeard is out goose hunting (and *bécasse* is also applied pejoratively to foolish women) the itinerant monk is after similar game in the person of Mme. Angèle, who has already been called *une dinde*.

The text is given an ordered appearance by causal and coordinating conjunctions, but these are often devoid of logic. This technique is particularly important in a story which purports to explain actions and motivations but which demonstrates the futility of such an attempt.[32] The use of money as a persuasive, if not altogether pertinent factor in decisions is not original with France. He puts a bribe on equal footing with due process in a description of Bluebeard's divorce proceedings:

> ...il demanda à Rome l'annulation d'un mariage qui n'était qu'un leurre, et l'obtint selon le droit canon et moyennant un beau présent au Saint-Père. (142)

Similarly, wealth is equated with appearance as an index of popularity:

> Pourtant, il est vrai qu'il ne plaisait pas aux dames autant qu'il aurait dû leur plaire, fait de la sorte et riche. (133)

In both cases, the clause introduced by *et* presents a tangential rather than a parallel argument.

The explanation of Angèle's behavior is cleverly convoluted for a licentious effect: "...et aussitôt l'innocente faisait, au gré des fripons qui voulaient d'elle ce qu'il était bien naturel d'en vouloir, car elle était jolie." (141) But the most striking example

---

[32] This technique is typical of the Voltairian *conte philosophique*.

of convoluted logic in the story is the tautology used to explain Bluebeard's appearance:

> En effet, sa barbe était bleue, mais elle n'était bleue que parce qu'elle était noire, et c'était à force d'être noire qu'elle était bleue.[33]

Finally, we can see a paradigm for France's technique of contrasting syntax and semantics in this sentence whose structure negates its meaning:

> Il laissait paraître sa préférence, qu'il n'avait pas à cacher, car elle était honnête; et d'ailleurs il était sans détours. (148)

In this example, straightforward honesty is expressed by a tortuous structure: *sans détours* (Bluebeard's intent) contrasts with the *détours* of his expression. The opposite phenomenon is produced in the description of Gigonne Aignel. Her twisted appearance is described in a symmetrical style, and the incongruity of this symmetry is emphasized by the elegant chiasmus which follows it:

> Assez belle fille, à cela près qu'elle louchait d'un œil et clochait d'un pied. Sitôt qu'elle fut épousée, cette gardeuse d'oies, mordue par une folle ambition, ne rêva plus que grandeurs nouvelles et nouvelles splendeurs. (138)

These narrative tricks reinforce, on a small scale, the story's larger concern with form and substance, description and reality.

In both theme and structure, then, "Les Sept Femmes de la Barbe-Bleue" exposes the shortcomings of modern historical methodology. The same facts can be used to build an image or destroy a reputation. More important than potential dishonesty, however, is the fundamental purpose of historical research. France's

---

[33] France, XIX, 133. This paradox had amused France for a long time. An earlier — and less effective — version of the *bleu-noir* paradox can be found in the *Dialogue:* "Raymond: Barbe-Bleue n'est pas aussi noir qu'on le fait. Laure: Pas aussi noir? Raymond: Il n'est pas noir du tout, puisque c'est le soleil." (France, III, 413).

Bluebeard has been called a murdered myth,[34] and indeed, he is a sheepish hero, robbed of all his prestige. As France says in *Le Jardin d'Epicure,* "si Barbe-Bleue n'avait pas tué ses femmes, son histoire en serait moins jolie."[35] Rehabilitation has made Bluebeard "real" but it has also destroyed his inherent beauty and strength.

Mythical heroes, even infamous villains, are part of our heritage; they reflect the first efforts of the human creative spirit. We can learn from them our basic aspirations and motivations. But France remains skeptical about the uses to which this knowledge can be put. We can learn what man is, but man does not change and self-knowledge serves no purpose. As the narrator says early in his tale:

> Ma grand'mère disait que l'expérience, dans la vie, ne sert à rien et qu'on reste ce qu'on était. Je crois qu'elle avait raison et l'histoire véritable que je retrace ici n'est pas pour lui donner tort. (149)

In spite of the narrator, or even because of him, Bluebeard remains what he is; and history remains the most elegant of our old wives' tales.

---

[34] Sister M. Madeleva, "Anatole France: Four parodies on Historical research," *University of California Chronicle,* XXIX, No. 1, (Jan. 1927), p. 10.

[35] France, *Le Jardin d'Epicure, Œuvres* (Paris: Calmann-Lévy, 1927), IX, 459. Hereafter referred to as *Epicure,* IX.

CHAPTER II

"LE GRAND SAINT NICOLAS"

Miracles, especially the lives of the saints, figure prominently in France's work.[1] These stories of suffering and transfiguration reflect the primary miracle of Christianity: Christ's resurrection. They were the stories France was raised on; they inspired him to plan a career as a professional "Ermite et Saint du Calendrier"[2] as a child and to compose the life of Sainte Radegonde at the age of fifteen. Sylvestre Bonnard, an early and popular Francian character, was a scholar of the *Legenda aurea,* the handbook of medieval saints, whose genesis he explains:

> La *Légende dorée* est par elle-même un vaste et gracieux ouvrage. Jacques de Voragine, définiteur de l'ordre de Saint Dominique et archevêque de Gênes, assembla, au XII⁰ siècle, les traditions relatives aux saints de la catholicité, et il en forma un recueil d'une telle richesse qu'on s'écria dans les monastères et dans les châteaux: 'C'est la légende dorée!'[3]

Bonnard's adventures in search of a rare manuscript are humorous; his pedantry and simplicity are amusing but not particularly ironic. France's treatment of the miracles and of the *légende dorée* is much more biting in his short stories.

---

[1] For a detailed study of the use of medieval material in France's work see Alvida Ahlstrom, *Le moyen Age dans l'œuvre d'Anatole France* (Paris: Les Belles Lettres, 1930).

[2] France, *Ami,* III, 243.

[3] France, *Le Crime de Sylvestre Bonnard, Œuvres* (Paris: Calmann-Lévy, 1925), II, 277. Hereafter cited as *Bonnard,* II.

Of all religious texts, these episodes are the most dramatic and the most susceptible to parody. They are tailored to the ironic mentality, the persistently double perception. The simple, naive faith of these martyrs appealed to France; he was capable of writing touching and sincere renditions of existing legends, such as "Le Christ de l'océan" or "Le Jongleur de Notre-Dame."[4] But at the same time, France could see the egotism, bigotry, and often poorly sublimated motivations of many religious zealots; as his critics have so often shown, France was essentially a champion of pagan, Hellenistic virtues.[5] He frequently mocks not only the simplicity or hypocrisy of his protagonists but that of readers who accept such stories as fact. It is significant that *Thaïs* and other religious stories such as "Amycus et Célestin" or "Saint-Satyr"[6] were originally subtitled "conte philosophique." The subtitle indicates the basically ironic goal of the stories: to enlighten rather than edify.

The tone of France's criticism varies from story to story. Often he has great indulgence for the miracle itself and reserves his irony for a pseudo-scholarly framework, as in the story of Saints Oliverie and Liberette. France felt that religious legends, particularly those of the early Gallic missionaries, were a valuable part of French cultural heritage and worthy of the attention of "tous ceux qui s'intéressent à l'histoire de notre pays."[7] But it is clear that their value does not lie in factual accuracy. The narrator of "Sainte Euphrosine," for example, realizes that the experts will find inconsistencies or errors in his story, but he defends himself in advance with the argument that "n'ayant qu'un seul texte, c'est celui-là que j'ai dû suivre. Il est en fort mauvais état et peu lisible. Mais il faut dire que tous les chefs-d'œuvre de l'antiquité classique, dont nous faisons nos délices, nous sont parvenus dans cet état."[8] Even if the manuscript were in good condition, there would be no way to guarantee the accuracy of the events it describes.

---

[4] In *L'Etui de Nacre* (V) and *Crainquebille* (XIV).

[5] "Ces pieux personnages n'ont pas fait périr le moindre petit dieu.... Les génies, les nymphes, et les fées se cachent quelquefois, mais ils ne meurent jamais. Ils défient le goupillon des saints." (France, *Pierre Nozière*, X, 435.)

[6] In *L'Etui de Nacre* (V) and *Le Puits de Sainte Claire* (X).

[7] France, *Pierre Nozière*, X, 435.

[8] France, *L'Etui de Nacre*, V, 276.

Legends are born easily, as France demonstrates in the creation of a local folk myth in "Putois"; [9] and seemingly "authentic" miracles can be counterfeited, as in "Le Miracle de la Pie." [10] And finally, even if the good works described in saint's legends are essentially correct, they often conceal ignorance, selfishness, or fanaticism. These failings range from the foolish, worldly vanity of Sainte Scolastica to the tortured carnal desires of Paphnuce or Brother Mino. [11]

The popularity of the legend of Saint Nicolas stretches across the centuries. The well-known story was included in the *Bibliothèque Bleue* (the original dime novels) of the early seventeenth century; the musical version was even used as the model for a political satire during the Boulanger scandal of the late nineteenth century. [12] France may have first considered using the story of Saint Nicolas when he reviewed the rhymed version of that tale written by the poet Gabriel Vicaire in October of 1889. In his review, he quotes the folklorist Paul Sébillot who laments the fact that French artists "ont dédaigné cette source d'inspiration." [13] France made extensive use of folk tales and legends, but not to the purpose which Sébillot had envisaged, and his version of Saint Nicolas is certainly very different from Vicaire's sentimental poem. Jean-Jacques Brousson tells of France's impulse to add an ironic ending to edifying legends: "J'ai quelquefois envie de donner un epilogue à ces légendes. Le méchant loup de Gubbio, vous le savez, est mort de vieillesse, et sa fin fut très edifiante..." [14] In the story of Saint Nicolas, it is a question of a different kind of wolf in sheep's clothing: a miracle that backfires.

The traditional story of the Bishop of Myra combines the two qualities of candor and inaccuracy which had so often served as foils for France's wit. The story is a weed among the "golden

---

[9] In *Crinquebille* (XIV).
[10] In *Les Contes de Jacques Tournebroche* (XIX).
[11] In *Thaïs* (V), and *Le Puits de Sainte Claire* (X).
[12] France writes in his article in *Le Temps* of May 11, 1890: "Rappelez-vous la *Perquisition* et les *Manifestations Boulangistes* sur l'air de la *Légende de Saint Nicolas:* 'Ils étaient trois petits garçons, Qui passaient, chantant des chansons...'" (France, *La Vie littéraire III*, VII, 374).
[13] *Ibid.*, 163.
[14] Jean-Jacques Brousson, *Anatole France en pantoufles* (Paris: Crès, 1926), p. 143.

flowers" of legend, conspicuously absent from Voragine's *Legenda Aurea*. This popular legend, which developed from a perceptual *malentendu* of the faithful,[15] is specifically not recognized by the Church and is therefore the perfect choice for an ironic defense of the veracity of legends.

The premise of the story of Saint Nicolas is exactly the reverse of that in France's tale of Bluebeard. In that story, France proved that an existing text was false; here, he proves that a nonexistant text is true. In both stories, however, the plot hinges on a case of mistaken identity, and the authority of the "real" figure is cleverly manipulated to authenticate the false one.

Saint Nicolas of Myra is an historical figure, a patron of children and a patriarch venerated by the Church — but he never performed the miracle of the triple resurrection. France solves the dilemma by coming up with a second Saint Nicolas:

> car il y en a deux; l'un, comme nous avons dit, évêque de Myre en Lycie; l'autre, moins ancien, évêque de Trinqueballe en Vervignole. Il m'en était réservé d'en faire la distinction. (169)

The narrator appears to take credit for the authenticity of the first bishop ("comme nous avons dit") and he uses this authority to establish the existence of the second; the two are thus linked psychologically as well as grammatically ("l'un...l'autre"). The parallel extends to their geographical location. "Myre in Lycie" did exist, even if few people could say exactly where; and thus the parallel structure "Trinqueballe en Vervignole" is potentially no more obscure, and receives a modicum of authenticity.

The Latin word *legenda* means "that which is to be read." As Lüthi points out, "It has not, like the fairy tale, been entrusted

---

[15] The Bishop of Myra is often depicted baptising three pagan converts. It was common in Byzantine iconography to portray the principal figure in larger dimensions than lesser characters. Simple copyists not acquainted with this tradition understandably mistook the pagans for children; and seeing inscriptions like the following: *Auxit mactados hic fonte renatos*, they confused the symbolic rebirth of baptism with a literal resurrection. Popular imagination gradually transformed the stone fount into a pork barrel and filled in the details of the adventure. See Alfred Maury, *Essai sur les légendes pieuses du Moyen-Age* (Paris: Ladrange, 1843) for a discussion of the origins and widespread popularity of this legend.

to those who transmit by word of mouth — the workers and servants — but has been written down, namely by clerics." [16] However, the "text" in question in the story of Saint Nicolas recalls the pseudo text presented by the narrator in the story of Bluebeard; it is simply the accumulated hearsay of the ages, "la complainte universellement connue," "la conscience populaire." (167-68) But like more orthodox texts, this legend "porte en lui les caractères inimitables de la candeur et de la bonne foi." (168) It is true that the description and indeed, even the circumstances of the miracle are presented in ironic or skeptical terms— and the many ironies of the story of Saint Nicolas will be discussed at length — but France does not dispute the basic facts of the miracle. The narrator's assertion is contextually accurate: "Le miracle du saloir est vrai, du moins en ce qu'il a d'essentiel," (169) and the three children are brought back to life through Divine intercession.

The most immediate precedent for the tale of Saint Nicolas in France's work is found in *L'Ile des Pingouins*. [17] In many ways, the short story is a condensation and refinement of themes which figure prominently in the novel: the dubious consequences of an act of faith, the unpredictable and disillusioning social development of the "saved," as well as France's standard barbs at historical accuracy.

Just as the three children are miraculously resurrected, the penguins of Penguin Island are transformed into men through the intercession of God. The fact of their transformation is not disputed in the context of the story, even though the circumstances surrounding their baptism are highly unorthodox. Both miracles of transformation are "true" in context; and in both stories the main interest centers on the consequences of the miracle, the author's ironic "epilogue."

An amusing contrast wtih these "true" miracles is provided by the travesty miracle of Saint Orberose and the dragon in *L'Ile des Pingouins*. Everyone acts on cue in this carefully staged production — including the credulous faithful. The "virgin" Orberose "s'avance vêtue de blanc sur la bruyère rose. D'un pas

---

[16] Lüthi, p. 37.
[17] Published serially in 1905-06.

intrépide et modeste elle marche vers la bête..." The "monster," "poussant des hurlements affreux, ouvre une gueule enflammée." The horrified crowd lets out "un immense cri de terreur et de pitié."[18] The virgin leashes the beast who is then slain by a long-lost hero, none other than Orberose's lover, Kraken. He slashes the monster's belly — whence appear "en chemise, les cheveux bouclés et les mains jointes, le petit Elo et les cinq autres enfants que le monstre avait dévorés."[19] The resurrected children kneel at the virgin's feet; she takes them in her arms and speaks softly to them, but her language is hardly appropriate to this touching tableau:

> Vous irez par les villages et vous direz: 'Nous sommes les pauvres petits enfants que le dragon a dévorés et nous sommes sortis en chemise de son ventre.' Les habitants vous donneront en abondance tout ce que vous pouvez souhaiter. Mais, si vous parlez autrement vous n'aurez que des nasardes et des fessées. Allez![20]

This miracle, which is bogus in context, is accepted with as much enthusiasm by the faithful as is the "real" miracle in the story of Saint Nicolas. And in fact, the Penguins are more justifiable; they are shown a much more convincing spectacle. The children look the part with their carefully curled hair, long white shirts and hands joined in prayer, and they recite their lines beautifully: "Nous sommes les pauvres petits enfants que le dragon a dévorés et nous sommes sortis en chemise de son ventre."[21] The people, suitably impressed, act as predicted and comically repeat Orberose's formula word for word: "Enfants bénis, nous vous donnerons en abondance tout ce que vous pourrez souhaiter."[22] On the contrary, the authentically miraculous children in the tale of Saint Nicolas are a tattered and scruffy crew: "Ils portaient encore les haillons dont ils étaient vêtus au jour de leur mort." They are described in terms more appropriate to a litter of puppies than God's chosen: *craintif, sauvage, robuste,*

---

[18] France, *Ile*, XVIII, 122.
[19] *Ibid.*
[20] *Ibid.*
[21] *Ibid.*, 123.
[22] *Ibid.*

*malingre.* Their behavior is scarcely edifying — "ces pauvres enfants ne savient que rire et tirer la langue." (181) But the will to believe is strong and the jubilant public interprets this behavior as "une preuve sensible de leur innocence et de leur misère." (181)

The false miracle in *L'Ile des Pingouins* results in happiness and prosperity for the future Sainte Orberose and tranquility in the land. But the *bona fide* miracles in *L'Ile des Pingouins* and "Saint Nicolas" result in ultimate failure and disillusionment for the holy men who wrought them and eventual disaster for the general population. Saint Nicolas is as blind as the myopic Saint Mael; both attempt to effect the transformation of creatures who are essentially imperfect, and both fail. The fault does not lie with God's miracles but rather with human nature.

Both stories deal with the debunking of a myth; not the miraculous *point de départ* but rather faith in human progress and perfectability. In each story, the miracle is quickly dispatched in the opening pages and the body of the story deals with the human ramifications.

The picture is unremittingly bleak in *L'Ile des Pingouins*. France follows the Penguin society through its successive stages of development: that is, through its increasing corruption. The miracle of rebirth turns out to be a colossal joke played on the Penguins by fate, as backhanded a gift as the little brass box in the anarchist fairy tale which closes their history:

> Un pêcheur, ayant jeté ses filets dans la mer, en tira un petit pot de cuivre fermé; il l'ouvrit avec son couteau. Il en sortit une fumée qui s'éleva jusqu'aux nues et cette fumée, en s'épaississant, forma un géant qui éternua si fort, si fort que le monde entier fut réduit en poussière...[23]

The moral is as old as Pandora and just as clear: the fisherman in his greed and curiosity unleashes his own destruction; and the new Penguin society which springs up after the holocaust follows exactly in the footsteps of the previous one.[24]

---

[23] France, *Ile*, XVIII, 410.
[24] France indicates this cyclical determinism by repeating the description of the society word for word.

The story of Saint Nicolas is in many ways an encapsulated version of *L'Ile des Pingouins*. Three boys are reborn rather than an entire people — but they represent the main scourges of civilization: war, religious fanaticism, and avarice; faults which they retained from their previous incarnation, hence the notion of recurring human imperfection. The children possess admirable character traits as well: prudence, courage, thoughtfulness; but they are perverted "par suite de la corruption commune à tout le genre humain." (184)

The principal movement and interest of the story of Saint Nicolas, however, is dialectical rather than cyclical. Levaillant has discussed the paradigm of contrasting parallels of passion and lucidity in *Thaïs*, another religious *conte philosophique*.[25] "Le Grand Saint Nicolas" presents the same pattern in parody form, since both the depth of the suffering and the horror of the perception have been eliminated. In *Thaïs*, Paphnuce denies his natural emotions (his love for the courtisan Thaïs) and thus distorts them; his obsession leads him to disaster. Nicolas is also led astray by a carnal emotion: his fondness for his niece, Mirande. "Les saints eux-mêmes ne savent pas toujours trancher les liens de la chair. Nicolas aimait sa nièce avec pureté, mais non sans délectation." (198) But while Paphnuce's internal conflict is purely sexual, France represents a more general conflict in "Le Grand Saint Nicolas" with the contrasting figure of Nicolas and the deacon, Modernus: Nicolas, the creature of emotion, and Modernus, a bastion of common sense.

Nicolas' basic goal is unselfish and laudable in principle. He wants to effect social reform through progressive amelioration and education. He finds the resurrected children in a woeful state of ignorance and plans to educate them "graduellement par l'application des meilleurs règles pédagogiques." (198) In his enthusiasm, however, he has no sense of measure; he wants the children to learn "les vérités nécessaires au salut... les arts libéraux, et, en particulier, la musique... la rhétorique, la philosophie et l'histoire des hommes, des animaux et des plantes." (182) Nicolas' theories are noble, but from the very beginning he demonstrates his total ineptitude for their practical application. He attempts to ask the

---

[25] See Levaillant, *Essai*, pp. 282-284.

children easy questions "proportionées à leur âge" and comes up with " 'Qu'est-ce que Dieu?' " (182) He wants the children to study the animals "dont tous les organes, par leur inconcevable perfection, attestent la gloire du Créateur," (182) but his own familiarity with anatomy is glaringly inadequate, and on a practical level he is far less knowledgeable than the boys:

> Nous rions, dit Maxime, de ce que vous prenez une jument pour un cheval. Vous n'en voyez pas la différence; elle est pourtant bien visible. Vous vous connaissez donc pas en animaux? (183)

In theory, Nicolas' ideas often appear quite reasonable. Few could argue with his precepts on educational techniques:

> Il convient de redresser leurs torts avec une longue patience et une obstinée douceur.... Redressons-les avec mille précautions, de peur d'augmenter le mal au lieu de le diminuer. (186)

Again, his general rule for child-rearing is accepted practice in liberal circles: "Les soins donnés à notre enfance nous font meilleurs. Une éducation trop dure nous durcit." (188) Unfortunately, all of Saint Nicolas' efforts are directed against subjects who are demonstrably incorrigible. Nicolas' fault lies in not recognizing, as Modernus points out, that "il n'y a pas de bonne éducation sans castoiement, ni discipline sans discipline." (187)

This particularly bitter satire of progressive education can be explained in part by France's disillusionment over the failure of the Universités Populaires in 1907 which epitomized the inability of intellectuals to communicate effectively with workers. Levaillant describes France's reaction as

> la brusque prise de conscience qu'entre la politique traditionnelle du socialisme et les réalités de l'évolution sociale, il existe un irréductible et mystérieux hiatus. Désarroi fondamental, contradiction entre l'humanisme impuissant à changer l'ordre des choses et la terreur catastrophique.[26]

---

[26] Levaillant, *Essai*, p. 683.

This apparently unbridgeable gap is the central theme of "Le Grand Saint Nicolas." France has skewed the structure of his story by ostensibly arriving at the climax — the miracle — after only a few pages. He then builds to the true climax, Nicolas' destruction, through a series of episodes situated within the point and counterpoint of Nicolas' and Modernus' opposing perceptions. Aside from the humor inherent in these contrasts, this structure prevents too rapid an accumulation of catastrophes which would result not only in a premature climax but would also inspire some pity in the reader for Nicolas. Modernus' running commentary on his actions leaves Nicolas without an excuse, even within the context of the story.

Modernus' pragmatism and Nicolas' simple faith and impracticality are established in the opening pages of the story, before the miracle of the pork barrel, when the deacon informs his master:

> Il ne me reste ni une goutte de vin ni une miette de pain, car j'ai tout donné, par votre ordre, sur la route, à des gens qui en avaient moins besoin que nous. (173)

Modernus' roots are definitely in the physical world, and because of this, during the miraculous revelation, "il ne vit pas l'ange, et il ne l'entendit pas, parce qu'il n'était pas assez saint pour communiquer avec les esprits célestes." [27] Moreover, Modernus' analysis of the boys' true nature is reinforced by very physical experiences — a dunking in the river and "une potée d'eau de vaisselle avec le pot, dont il eut le crâne fêlé." (190) Nicolas, on the contrary, steadfastly refuses to accept empirical evidence.

Modernus analyzes the facts and makes logical conclusions. In contrast with Nicolas' impractical educational schemes, Modernus merely observes the boys' actual unsocialized condition and concludes "qu'il faut d'abord apprendre à ces enfants la civilité." (183) After a long enumeration of the children's pranks (ranging from the mischievous to the sadistic), Nicolas blithely predicts, "Ils deviendront de fidèles serviteurs de Dieu et leurs mérites

---

[27] France, XIX, 178. Modernus resembles the disciple of the Egyptian monk, Schnoudi, who conversed with Christ. See France, *La Vie littéraire*, *III*, VII, 138 ff.

seront comptés." (184) In contrast, when Maxime throws the deacon in the river, Robin steals his ring and Sulpice sees a devil ready to snatch his soul, Modernus correctly and succinctly predicts that the boys will turn out "l'un cupide, l'autre violent, le troisième visionnaire," (186) and he warns the bishop, "Si vous ne punissez pas ces trois mauvais garnements, ils deviendront pires qu'Hérode." (187) Finally, when Modernus observes that "Sulpice est capable d'outrer jusqu'à l'hérésie la soumission à l'Eglise," (206) Nicolas criticises him for lacking Christian charity, failing to realize that charity begins at home.

Nicolas' emotional and unthinking reactions result in both personal and professional ruin. The episodes which lead to his destruction are general at first but become more and more specific. Nevertheless, Nicolas remains oblivious to the gradually tightening circle until it is too late. The boys' corruption develops all too quickly. Robin first learns the ropes of money-lending, then forecloses on the personal fortune of Nicolas' niece, Mirande, and finally sells Nicolas' debts, resulting in the desecration of the cathedral; Maxime corrupts the village girls and goes on to devastate the countryside as a military hero, rape Mirande and finally sack the cathedral; Sulpice leads the town's young people into heresy, then corrupts the monks of the local monastery and finally Mirande. These blows lead Nicolas himself into disobediance and disgrace.

The public and private aspects of Nicolas' life are represented by the cathedral of Trinqueballe (and specifically by the patron saint, Gibbosine) and his niece, Mirande. France has established many parallels between the two, and Nicolas' destruction proceeds on the two levels simultaneously. Nicolas is devoted to the Church and adores his niece but his indulgence and lack of judgment leads them both into ruin. Both Mirande and the Church exist in a vulnerable state of ignorance. Like Sainte Gibbosine,[28] Mirande inspires respect which, unfortunately, is her only protection against the audacious, impious, or heretical:

---

[28] "Depuis trois cents ans ses yeux d'émail, grands ouverts sur sa face d'or, frappaient d'un respect les habitants de Trinqueballe..." (France, XIX, 202.)

> Nulle vierge, en toute la Vervignole, n'inspirait tant de respect et nulle n'avait plus besoin d'en inspirer, car elle était merveilleusement simple, crédule, et sans défense. (197)

Both Mirande and Sainte Gibbosine are greedy, despite their virtue; their tastes are not as simple as their minds. Mirande distributes alms but buys expensive jewels and clothing; Sainte Gibbosine menaces the sleeping parishoners with "de maux très cruels s'ils ne lui donnaient en quantité suffisante de la cire vierge et des écus de six livres." (197) Nicolas seems to foster this extravagance: he dispenses his wealth to the poor on a lavish scale and goes into debt rather than curb his generosity or diminish the Church's stock of valuable ornaments. The creditors, however, are singularly lacking in respect either for Nicolas or for the Church, and the bishop is powerless to save either his niece or his cathedral from destitution. Mirande is distraught when her possessions are confiscated, but she is still capable of giving as shrewd a description of each item as one would find in a dealer's catalog:

> Il m'a pris, dit-elle en gémissant, mes corps et mes jupes de velours, de brocart et de dentelle, mes diamants, mes émeraudes, mes saphirs, mes jacinthes, mes améthystes, mes rubis, mes grenats, mes turquoises; il m'a pris ma grande croix de diamants à têtes d'anges en émail, mon grand carcan, composé de deux tables de diamants, de trois cabochons et de six nœuds de quatre perles chacun; il m'a pris mon grand collier de treize tables de diamants avec vingt perles en poire sur ouvrage à cantille... (199)

The same kind of ironic inventory is expanded in the scene where the cathedral is stripped of its decorations and treasures, culminating in an amusingly literal dismemberment:

> Seligman, Issichar et Meyer enlevèrent les chasses d'or ornées de pierreries, d'émaux et de cabochons, les reliquaires en forme de coupe, de lanterne, de nef, de tour, les autels portatifs en albâtre encadrés d'or et d'argent, les coffrets émaillés par les habiles ouvriers de Limoges et du Rhin, les croix d'autel, les évangelicaires recouverts d'ivoire sculptée et de camées antiques, les peignes liturgiques ornés de festons de pampres, les diptyques consu-

> laires, les pyxides, les chandeliers, les candélabres, les lampes, dont ils soufflaient la sainte lumière et versaient l'huile bénite sur les dalles; les lustres semblables à de gigantesques couronnes, les chapelets aux grains d'ambre et de perles, les colombes eucharistiques, les ciboires, les calices, les patènes, les baisers de paix, les navettes à encens, les burettes, les ex-voto sans nombre, pieds, mains, bras, jambes, yeux, bouches, entrailles, cœurs en argent, et le nez du roi Sidoc et le sein de la reine Blandine, et le chef en or massif de monseigneur Saint Cromadaire, premier apôtre de Vervignole et benoît patron de Trinqueballe. (201)

France reinforces the parallel between the two scenes by using the same verb — *gémir* — to describe both Mirande and Sainte Gibbosine during their respective traumas: Mirande speaks "en gémissant" (199) while "Sainte Gibbosine gémit, trembla, chancela sur son socle, et se laissa emporter sans résistance..." (202)

Mirande offers a similar lack of resistance to the returning conqueror, Maxime; and in an amusing and extended syllepsis he rapes Mirande and sacks the cathedral. As a last blow to Nicolas, his own niece becomes the major disciple of Sulpice's heretical sect, Edenism. This doctrine of original innocence flourishes in the climate of simple credulity which Nicolas has fostered. When he finally realizes what has transpired, he might just as well speak of his dioces or his cathedral as his niece when he laments:

> J'avais une nièce florissante de beauté, de vertu, de piété, et les trois enfants que j'ai tirés du saloir l'ont réduite à l'état misérable où je la vois. L'un la dépouille de tous ses biens, source abondante d'aumônes, patrimoine des pauvres; un autre lui ôte l'honneur; le troisième la rend hérétique.[29]

For the first time, Nicolas can appreciate the irony of his situation. The children he rescued have caused his ruin.

---

[29] France, XIX, 208. Mirande's sad end is a parody of the last days of Joan of Arc, emprisoned and tormented by the idea that she was sinning by wearing a dress: "ce qui l'affligeait le plus, c'est qu'on lui avait mis de force une vieille cotte et un chaperon et qu'elle n'était plus sûre de ne pas pécher." (France, XIX, 210).

France uses references to the *saloir* as a leitmotiv throughout the story. The refrain emphasizes the unremitting progression of Nicolas' downfall. It is doubly ironic the first time Nicolas refers to the miracle because he is completely naive: "Je suis heureux, disait le saint évêque Nicolas, d'avoir tiré ces enfants du saloir pour en faire de bons chrétiens." (184) The reader is already wiser than Nicolas, since the preceeding list of the children's pranks is ample proof of the contrary. Nicolas ironically links each new crisis with the original miracle; the contrast implies both the boys' incorrigibility and the indifference of Divine providence:

> Hélas, lui dit-il, *vous ai-je tiré du saloir* pour la perte des vierges de Vervignole? [30]
>
> Seigneur, *n'avez-vous tiré celui-ci du saloir* que comme un loup ravissant pour dévorer ma brebis? [31]
>
> Nicolas... lui représenta que *Dieu ne l'avait pas tiré du saloir* pour attenter aux biens de notre sainte mère l'Eglise. (192)
>
> Et il pria pour les affligés et notamment pour Robin *qu'il avait, par la volonté de Dieu, tiré du saloir.* (202)

The same refrain is used humorously by Modernus, reinforcing the story's dialectical structure. Modernus, with his typical lucidity, predicts the consequences of Robin's business finesse:

> Soyez certain que *ce Robin, que vous avez tiré du saloir,* s'entend, pour vous dépouiller, avec les Lombards du Pont Vieux et les juifs du Ghetto, et qu'il se réserve la plus grosse part du butin. (195)

Nicolas' laments, on the contrary, are consistently *ex post facto*.

As we have seen, the story of Saint Nicolas is built on an accumulation of disasters which lead to the final disillusionment of the protagonist. This development is accented by the *leitmotiv*

---

[30] France, XIX, 190. Italics here and in the following citations mine.

[31] *Ibid.*, 204. Cf. Saint Abraham and his niece Marie in *La Vie littéraire*, III: "Un loup cruel a enlevé ma brebis'." (France, VII, 229). Nicolas frequently expresses himself in such religious clichés.

of the *saloir*. It is reinforced on a syntactical level as well by the use of the stylistic devices of enumeration, pleonasm, hyperbole and climax. Bresky has commented on France's use of these techniques, drawing many examples from "Le Grand Saint Nicolas." He correctly points out the intrinsic humor of these passages, but fails, however, to point out the relationship underlying these passages and their context. For example, he quotes the enumeration which figures in the devil's description of the *saloir* (immediately preceeding the miracle):

> Il le reçut des mains d'un habile tonnelier, le parfuma de genièvre, de thym et de romarin. Le seigneur Garum n'a pas son pareil pour saigner la chair, la désoser, la découper, curieusement, studieusement, amoureusement, et l'imprégner des esprits salins qui la conservent et l'embaument. Il est sans rival pour assaisoner, concentrer, réduire, écumer, tamiser, décanter la saumure. (177)

Bresky concludes, "It achieves its amusing effect without the climax by the grotesque chain of bizarre culinary techniques." [32] More importantly, the essential characteristic of this Rabelaisian enumeration is its verbal intoxication. It must appear to be an uncontrolled outpouring of words, one word summoning the next with a nearly incantatory effect. The reader is not only amused but also inebriated and slightly hypnotized by the flow. The technique is thus perfectly suited to illustrate the temptation of the saint by the devil.

The many climactic and pleonastic passages in the story intensify the basic cumulative development of the plot. France varies his technique, since any humorous device becomes tiresome with repetition. For example, a rapid crescendo of verbs expresses the immediate action demanded by the Church hierarchy:

> Il invita de la façon la plus instante, par lettres scellées de son sceau, le seigneur évêque Nicolas à *appréhender, incarcérer, interroger* et *juger*, de concert avec lui, ces ennemis de Dieu... (209; italics mine)

---

[32] Bresky, 56.

The triumph of the hypocrite, Robin, is described with a more complicated crescendo effect:

> Il apportait cette fâcheuse nouvelle à son bienfaiteur avec la politesse obséquieuse qui lui était ordinaire; mais il se montrait bien moins affligé qu'il n'eût dû l'être en cette extrémité douloureuse. De fait, il avait grand'peine à dissimuler sous une mine allongée son humeur allègre et sa vive satisfaction. Le parchemin de ses jaunes, sèches, et humbles paupières cachait mal la lueur de joie qui jaillissant de ses prunelles aiguës. (195)

Robin progresses from *politesse obséquieuse* to *humeur allègre* and *vive satisfaction*. Because he is dishonest and concealing his true emotions, he is described in terms of a progressive revelation or unmasking. Beneath his politeness, he seems *moins affligé* than he should; under his *mine allongée* one can glimpse his true feelings; and his eyelids literally act as shades *(parchemin, jaunes, sèches)* which poorly conceal his uncontrolable joy.

The cumulative passages further reflect the basic movement of the story (Nicolas' progressive decline through a series of ironic oppositions) by the use of frequent contrasts employing a decrescendo or anticlimax. The most outrageously pleonastic passage in the story is Sulpice's frenzied declaration of obedience to the Church:

> Je déplore, je répudie, je condamne, je réprouve, je déteste, j'exècre, j'abomine mes erreurs passées, présentes et futures, dit-il; je me soumets à l'Eglise pleinement et entièrement, totalement et généralement, purement et simplement, et n'ai de croyance que sa croyance, de foi que sa foi, de connaissance que sa connaissance; je ne vois, n'entends, ni ne sens que par elle. Elle me dirait que cette mouche qui vient de se poser sur le nez du diacre Modernus est un chameau, qu'incontinent, sans dispute, contestation ni murmure, sans résistance, hésitation ni doute, je croirais, je déclarerais, je proclamerais, je confesserais, dans les tortures et jusqu'à la mort, que c'est un chameau qui s'est posé sur le nez du diacre Modernus. (205)

The first series is climactic: *déplore, répudie, condamne, réprouve* etc., followed by the progressive series *erreurs passées, présentes et futures.* The following series is a decrescendo: *pleinement et entièrement, totalement et généralement, purement et simplement,* followed by two more declining series: *sans dispute, contestation ni murmure, sans résistance, hésitation ni doute.* The passage ends with a rousing crescendo *(je croirais, je déclarerais...)* culminating in the ultimate limit of hyperbole *(dans les tortures et jusqu'à la mort).* After such sublime fervor, the final image appears as a ridiculous anticlimax. In a similar manner, the wrath of the Holy Father in Rome is undermined by the anticlimactic ending to his list of epithets. The vernacular *vieille femme* and *olibrius* follow the grandiloquent climax of *corrupteur des peuples:*

> Le Pape fulmina contre lui la bulle *maleficus pastor,* dans laquelle le vénérable pontife était traité de désobéissant, d'hérétique ou fleurant l'hérésie, de concubinaire, d'incestueux, de corrupteur des peuples, de vieille femme et d'olibrius, et véhémentement admonesté. (209)

Nicolas' helplessness is graphically conveyed in the contrast of his progressively stronger attempts to stem the disaster with an introductory (and undermining) adverb:

> En vain le grand saint Nicolas avertissait ses ouailles, exhortait, menaçait, fulminait. (207)

The impression of impotence is made even stronger by the adjective *le grand* which is placed in immediate opposition to *en vain.* The same kind of contrast is presented even more dramatically in Nicolas' confrontation with the foreclosing money-lenders:

> Alors, il les pria, les supplia, leur promit de payer sitôt qu'il le pourrait, au double, au triple, au décuple, au centuple, la dette dont ils étaient acquéreurs. Ils s'excusèrent poliment de ne pouvoir différer leur petite opération. L'évêque les menaça de faire sonner le tocsin, d'ameuter contre eux le peuple qui les tuerait comme des chiens en les voyant profaner, violer, dérober les images miraculeuses et les saintes reliques. Ils montrèrent en souriant les sergents qui les gardaient. (200)

Nicolas is helpless; his pleonastic promises and threats are pitiful. They seem particularly inflated in opposition to the understated

Jews who euphemistically refer to their *petite opération* and do not even waste their breath on an explanation.

Verbal accumulations are not the only striking stylistic techniques in the story. Just as pleonasm is used to dramatize Nicolas' impotence, France frequently reinforces character traits or situation with stylistic effects. For example, the difference in the personalities of Modernus and Nicolas is reflected in this early description of the two:

> Or, une fois qu'il avait chevauché sur sa mule, depuis l'aube, en compagnie du diacre Modernus, à travers les bois sombres, hantés du lynx et du loup, et les sapins antiques qui hérissent les sommets des monts Marmouse, l'homme de Dieu pénétra, au tomber du jour, dans des halliers épineux où sa monture se frayait difficilement un chemin sinueux et lent. Le diacre Modernus le suivait à grand'peine sur sa mule, qui portait le bagage. (173)

The sentence devoted to Nicolas is as "sinueux et lent" as the path; it is filled with poetic assonances *(lynx et loup; sombres, sapins, hérissent, sommets; sommets, monts, Marmouse, l'homme)* and romantic images *(sapins antiques, tomber du jour, sommet des monts)*. This high-blown style is contrasted with the prosaic description of Modernus. His "suivait à grand'peine sur sa mule" is on a distinctly more vernacular level than Nicolas' "sa monture se frayait difficilement un chemin"; and he is not concerned with atmosphere but with the baggage.

In the scene of the miracle, the apparition of the angel is described in a peculiarly disjointed sentence:

> Et un ange du ciel apparut, resplendissant de lumière, à Nicolas, et lui dit: (178)

The heavenly light suddenly appears suspended between the elements of the disjointed phrase "apparut... à Nicolas," and the biblical "et" which introduces the sentence adds to the miraculous atmosphere of the apparition.

France frequently uses disjointed sentences or sentences with multiple verbs and/or objects to give an impression of chaos, as in the following description of Mirande's ransacked room:

> L'évêque y trouva sa nièce accroupie sur le plancher, échevelée, les yeux brillants de larmes, près d'un coffre ouvert et vide, dans la salle en désordre. (198)

Another example of form imitating content is the description of Mirande's desolation over her lost possessions:

> Alors, tournant vers lui ses regards désolés, elle lui conta avec mille soupirs que Robin, Robin échappé du saloir, Robin si mignon, lui ayant dit maintes fois que, si elle avait envie d'une robe, d'une parure, d'un joyau, il lui prêterait avec plaisir l'argent nécessaire pour l'acheter, elle avait eu recours assez souvent à son obligeance, qui semblait inépuisable, mais que, ce matin même, un juif nommé Seligman était venu chez elle avec quatre sergents, lui avait présenté les billets signés par elle à Robin, et que, comme elle manquait d'argent pour les payer, il avait emporté toutes les robes, toutes les coiffures, tous les bijoux qu'elle possédait. (198)

This endless sentence is not a direct quote, and yet the indirect style is a perfect representation of the hysterical girl who rambles on pausing for breath at each of the numerous commas (the *mille soupirs* of the text), and petulantly repeating the culprit's name and the extent of her loss (*toutes les robes, toutes les coiffures, tous les bijoux*).

In much the same way that style is an integral component of the structure of the plot, France's irony appears on three distinct levels in the story of "Le Grand Saint Nicolas." His treatment of the saint's legend as a genre is clearly ironic: the edifying tale is used to disillusion. The situation within the tale is ironic: the dramatic irony of Nicolas' blindness to his circumstances. These ironies are strengthened or repeated by numerous ironic details in the narration. All of these ironies underline the structure basic to all the stories in the collection: the disproportion between cause and effect, expectation and reality, theory and application.

France discusses the evolution of the saint's legend as a genre in *L'Ile des Pingouins*: "Le mot de légende, qui indiquait d'abord ce que le fidèle doit lire, impliqua bientôt l'idée de fables pieuses et de contes puérils."[33] The process of "fabulisation" is acceler-

---

[33] France, *Ile*, XVIII, 178.

ated in the tale of Saint Nicolas. France ostensibly provides the story with all the earmarks of authenticity, but at he same time he indicates that it is merely a *conte puéril*. Unlike fairy tales, saint's legends abound in specific details. France provides ample (albeit unverifiable) local color. For example:

> En ce moment-là, le roi *Berlu* dans la *quatorzième* année de son règne, assemblait une puissante armée pour combattre les *Mambourniens*, obstinés ennemis de son royaume.... (190; italics mine)

The atmosphere of legend is further enhanced by superstitious details:

> ... la table dressée pour les repas était si longue que ceux qui se tenaient à l'un des bouts la voyaient se perdre au loin en une pointe indistincte, et, quand on y allumait des flambeaux, *elle rappelait la queue de la comète apparue en Vervignole pour annoncer la mort du roi Comus.* (172; italics mine)

Archaisms such as *roide* or *vérécondieux* add to the ambiance, as does pious narration, such as: "Une pensée lui vint, suggérée sans doute par le diable." (191) Like other celebrated evangelists before him, Saint Nicolas is fond of parable and draws instructive lessons from nature: the homily of the overburdened mare and the barren vine.[34]

The most important episode of the story, however — the miracle — is related in a style reminiscent of local legend or fairy tale rather than a true saint's legend.[35] The household devils France describes are familiar and irreverent, like the elves in Nodier's *Trilby*:

> En ce temps-là, les démons se mêlaient bien plus intimement qu'aujourd'hui à la vie domestique. Ils hantaient les maisons; blottis dans la boîte au sel, dans le pot au beurre ou dans quelque autre retraite, ils épiaient les gens et guettaient l'occasion de les tenter et de les induire en mal. Les anges aussi faisaient alors parmi les chrétiens des apparitions plus fréquentes. (177)

---

[34] See France, XIX, 183; 187-188.
[35] Local legends deal with the supernatural rather than the divine; they perturb rather than soothe. See Lüthi, *Once Upon a Time*.

The devil who tempts Saint Nicolas is a humorous imp, "gros comme une noisette" (177) who comes to an amusingly appropriate end:

> le petit diable, comme une châtaigne qu'on a jetée au feu sans la fendre, éclata avec un bruit horrible et une grande puanteur. (177)

In the saint's legend the divine world intrudes into the everyday world and inspires the reader with the conviction that these inexplicable events are part of some greater meaning. But in France's story the sacred becomes profaned by its contact with the world of men. The narrator assures the reader that thanks to the facts culled from his "documents authentiques," "l'on n'aura pas à déplorer la fin d'une légende." (169) Just the opposite is the case: the facts will kill the legend. The reconciliation of legend and fact of which the narrator is so proud —

> Aussi, n'est-ce pas sans une vive satisfaction que j'ai trouvé moyen de concilier l'autorité de la complainte avec le silence des anciens biographes du pontife lycien. (168)

is a sham. Reconciliation is a process of logic and miracles are a product of faith. The miraculous either transforms and uplifts or is itself compromised by the profane. By extending the story of the miracle of the resurrection into the realm of the everyday human world, France has forced the divine into a context where it cannot survive. Levaillant summarizes his strategy:

> Ou bien Dieu, pur et absolu, reste en dehors du monde, et risque fort de ne pas exister; ou bien, ramené à l'intérieur du monde, l'absolu est ramené à de tels accidents, à de tels mélanges, qu'il n'a aucune chance de conserver sa pureté: c'est-à-dire encore qu'il n'existe pas.[36]

The story of Saint Nicolas is divided into two sections in France's tale. First, the narrator's discussion and summary of the miracle; followed by a more detailed narration of the miraculous events along with their consequences. The introduction establishes

---

[36] Levaillant, *Essai*, 377.

the ironic treatment of the story that will follow; the legend is presented as an authentic miracle and is simultaneously desanctified. As an additional irony, it is the narrator's overzealousness which compromises the miracle. He insists on a literal interpretation of all the incidents recounted in the legend. The source of the story — a popular song — is taken as a text which must be accepted as gospel:

> Ce texte fameux dit expressément qu'un charcutier cruel mit les innocents "au saloir comme pourceaux." C'est-à-dire apparemment qu'il les conserva, coupés par morceaux, dans un bain de saumure. (168)

The salting down of the dismembered children is accepted literally: "En effect, c'est ainsi que s'opère la salaison du porc." (168) Therefore, when the events of the miracle contradict normal usage, there is reason for surprise. The narrator stresses the length of the curing process, ostensibly to contrast the unusual duration of this instance with normal procedures, thus enhancing the impact of the miracle:

> mais on est surpris de lire ensuite que les trois petits enfants restèrent sept ans dans la saumure, tandis qu'à l'ordinaire on commence au bout de six semaines environ à retirer du baquet, avec une fourchette de bois, les morceaux de chair. Le texte est formel: ce fut sept années après le crime que, selon la complainte, le grand saint Nicolas entra dans l'auberge maudite. (168)

But instead of heightening the sense of the miraculous, the lengthy technical analysis serves as preparation for the ironic play on words which undermines the climax — the moment of resurrection:

> Aussitôt, par l'imposition des mains sur le saloir, l'homme de Dieu ressuscita les *tendres victimes*. (168; italics mine)

In an authentic religious context, the clichés "l'homme de Dieu" and "tendres victimes" would be effective symbolic language. But in the literal context which France has established, any metaphorical interpretation of *tendres* has been rendered impossible; the scene is grotesque instead of inspiring. Martyrs are supposed to come through their trials unscathed. The children's "tenderization" seriously compromises the miracle's powers of edification; yet this is the *récit* which the narrator offers for the reader's "plaisir et profit." (169)

This technique is extended throughout the body of the story by ironic contrasts between literal and figurative meanings. For example, the cliché used to describe the boys' harmful influence on Mirande is completely reinfused with literal meaning:

> Ils lui enseignaient des façons et des termes qui sentaient l'hôtellerie et le saloir. (185)

France's humor ranges from the erudite to the equivocal. He treats a figurative obscenity with mock seriousness, and discusses the metonyme in the epithet "cul de bique":

> Elle appelait, sur leur exemple, la respectable dame Basine vieille bique, et même, prenant la partie pour le tout, cul de bique. (185)

Syllogisms provide similar contrasts between abstract and concrete meanings. France describes the abduction of the "vierges échevelées" of the "ville de Grosse-Nattes" who, both ravished and delighted, refuse to return home:

> Mais quand les pères, frères et fiancés de ces filles ravies vinrent les chercher, elles refusèrent de retourner au pays natal, alléguant qu'elles y sentiraient trop de honte, et préférant cacher leur déshonneur dans les bras qui l'avaient causé. (189)

The verb *alléguant* leaves no doubt as to the correct interpretation of *ravies*.

The dominant irony in the re-telling of the legend is the irony of situation: the basic chiasmic structure which Levaillant indicates in *Thaïs* — the blind seer, the lost savior. Nicolas can see the angel of God but he is blind to the actions of men; he saves the children and is lost, while the murderer receives heavenly grace. Nicolas had faith in the secret designs of divine providence. His trust and confidence is established before the miracle:

> Mais puisque tu n'as plus rien, c'est que Dieu l'a voulu, et sûrement il l'a voulu pour notre bien et profit. Il est possible qu'il nous cache à jamais les raisons de ce bienfait; peut-être, au contraire, nous les fera-t-il bientôt paraître. (173)

This is an attitude of orthodox optimism; blind acceptance, like the young Candide's, that there is an adequate reason for everything on this earth, even evil. At first Nicolas' faith provides an ironic contrast with the ills which beset him for the reader alone; his own faith remains unshaken:

> Dieu, dit-il, saura bien rétablir nos affaires penchantes. Il ne laissera pas renverser la maison qu'il a bâtie. (195)

Gradually, however, his confidence falters. The beginnings of doubt are expressed by a qualifying "mais":

> Votre sagesse est adorable; mais vos voies sont obscures et vos desseins mystérieux.[37]

Finally, in the climactic confrontation with Garum, the ex-murderer turned hermit, Nicolas apprehends the full irony of their situation (reinforced by the opposition *mis/tirés*) and dares to ask why his expectations have been frustrated and why he has received evil for good:

> Je loue Dieu qui vous accorda la paix du cœur après le meurtre horrible de trois enfants que vous avez mis dans le saloir comme pourceaux; mais moi, hélas! pour les en avoir tirés, ma vie a été remplie de tribulations, mon âme abreuvée d'amertume, mon épiscopat entièrement désolé. J'ai été déposé, excommunié par le père commun des fidèles. Pourquoi suis-je puni si cruellement de ce que j'ai fait? (213)

---

[37] France, XIX, 204. Nicolas' repeated trust in God is a dramatic expansion of a similar situation in *L'Ile des Pingouins*. The virtuous monk, Oddul, is punished for his virtue. The heaping of abuse on Nicolas has been developed figuratively; it is quite literal in Oddul's case: "Oddul se sentit violemment poussé dehors. A peine était-il descendu dans la rue qu'une main lui versa un pot de chambre sur la tête; et il songea: —Tes desseins sont mystérieux, seigneur, et tes voies impénétrables." (France, *Ile*, XVIII, 131).

Nicolas' query is made even more pathetic by the ironic juxtaposition of "paix du cœur" and "meurtre horrible."

Ironic disproportion, either between cause and effect or reality and perception, is reflected in many humorous details of the action. Things simply do not work the way they should. The city of Trinqueballe welcomes its victorious army and is sacked by its own conquering heros:

> L'armée victorieuse entra dans la ville de Trinqueballe, toute pavoisée et fleurie en son honneur, et dans cette illustre capitale de la Vervignole fit un grand nombre de viols, de pillages, de meurtres et d'autres cruautés, incendia plusieurs maisons, saccagea les églises, et prit dans la cathédrale tout ce que les juifs y avaient laissé, ce qui, à vrai dire, était peu de chose. (203)

The senseless vandalism of the cathedral is even more ironic since there is so little worth stealing. The action is both morally and logically absurd. As another example of ironic disproportion, Sulpice's doctrine of spotless purity results in filth and degradation:

> Bientôt Sulpice enseigna la doctrine de la pureté parfaite, que rien ne peut souillir, et le couvent de bons frères devint semblable à une cage de singes. (207)

In fact, Sulpice's talents are much more developed than they ought to be: "Il péchait en esprit; il errait en matières de foi avec une précocité surprenante; à l'âge où l'on n'a pas encore d'idées, il abondait en idées fausses." [38] Sulpice's disproportionate capacity for heresy is emphasized by the humorous contrast, "Je vous ai vu... renouveler avant votre *vingtième année douze siècles* d'opinions singulières." (205; italics mine) But if Sulpice's talents are surprisingly overproductive, Nicolas is humorously undereffective. The venerable pontif exercises his wrath to no avail; his antagonists are not Christian and are therefore immune to his anger:

---

[38] France, XIX, 191. France was apparently fond of this paradox; he reworked several variants of it, for example, "Il faut bien penser avant que de penser. Car ensuite il est trop tard..." (*Ile*, XVIII, 200) or "Mon petit garçon a perdu la raison à âge où l'on n'en a pas encore." (*Ami*, III, 243).

> Le saint homme leur jeta un regard qui eût foudroyé trois chrétiens. (200)

The epithet "le saint homme" is ironic in this context of religious impotence. Similarly, the epithet "le vénérable pontif" or "le saint homme" is ironic in a context of disgrace:

> Le pape fulmina contre lui la bulle *Maleficus pastor,* dans laquelle le vénérable pontif était traité de désobéissant, d'hérétique ou fleurant l'hérésie, de concubinaire, d'incestueux, de corrupteur de peuple, de vielle femme et d'olibrius.
>
> Foudroyé par le vicaire de Jésus-Christ, abreuvé d'amertume, accablé de douleur, le saint homme Nicolas descendit sans regret de son siège illustre... (209-10)

As in the story of Blue Beard, France uses the Voltarian technique of establishing epithets as clichés in "neutral" contexts. The humor of this technique lies not merely in repetition but in repetition in an incongruous context which underlines the automatic and mechanical aspect of the epithet.[39]

These recurring epithets are not the only incongruous descriptions in the text. France frequently uses ironic oxymorons to qualify characters or situations. Maxime's horse, for example, is "une jument assez bonne, à cela près qu'elle était borgne et boiteuse." (190) In a more complicated ironic contrast, France sandwiches the seemingly innocent statement "Au demeurant, c'étaient de simples enfants," (184) between a frank analysis of the boys' warped characters and an enumeration of their perverse behavior.

The only answer in the text to Nicolas' call for an explanation of the cosmic irony is the Voltairian "Adorons Dieu, dit Garum, et ne lui demandons pas de comptes." (213) Levaillant has discussed these echos of *Zadig* in the story of Saint Nicolas.[40] Zadig criticizes the messenger of God for killing a child who would have grown up to be a murderer: divine intervention in the world causes an immediate evil for ultimate good. France reverses the

---

[39] See Sareil, *Essai sur Candide,* (Genève: Droz, 1967).
[40] See Levaillant, *Essai,* 727n.

circumstance — but the end result is the same in both cases: the philosophical "mais."

France's conclusion, however, is more parodic than philosophical. Although the story contains a large dose of determinism, cosmic irony is not completely to blame for Nicolas' downfall. He is responsible for his own ruin insofar as he is blinded to the truth by his emotions. It is a final irony that Mirande "lui était plus chère que la lumière de ses yeux." (184) This pious cliché is unfortunately true; the bishop's fondness for his niece is excessive and interferes with his judgment. France emphasizes Nicolas' weakness by prefacing the description of his sentiments with two qualifications which would normally preclude them: his official position and his blood relationship:

> Le pieux évêque Nicolas, son oncle, la chérissait chaque jour davantage, et s'attachait à elle plus qu'on ne doit s'attacher aux créatures. Sans doute il l'aimait en Dieu, mais distinctement; il se plaisait en elle; il aimait à l'aimer; c'était sa seule faiblesse. (198)

Regardless of their crimes, Nicolas refuses to prosecute Mirande and Sulpice: "Nicolas éluda l'injonction, protesta de son obéissance, et n'obéit pas." (209) His ultimate disgrace thus stems from his self-indulgence and obstinacy.

By largely confining his irony to human dimensions, France's story joins the miracle and the philosophical tale and makes both genres the victim of his wit. Neither Nicolas' simple faith nor Graum's philosophical resignation próvide a satisfying moral for the story. France never allows Nicolas to learn the most important lesson to be drawn from his experiences: his own responsibility.

CHAPTER III

"L'HISTOIRE DE LA DUCHESSE DE CICOGNE ET DE M. DE BOULINGRIN QUI DORMIRENT CENT ANS EN COMPAGNIE DE LA BELLE AU BOIS DORMANT"

An orthodox skeptic makes no attempt to disentangle illusion from reality. He does not pose questions since he knows that definitive answers will always remain beyond man's grasp. Pyrrho, according to France,

> enseignait que les choses sont toutes également incertaines et discutables. Rien, disait-il, n'est intelligible. Nous ne devons nous fier ni aux sens ni à la raison. Il faut douter de tout et être indifférent à tout. Il ne subtilisait pas. [1]

For France, such a categorical stance was suspect. His own skepticism did not lead him to reject the world but rather to regard it with bemused detachment. In the tradition of French *philosophes*, France found a total suspension of belief and action unacceptable. "Faut-il donc agir? Sans doute qu'il le faut." [2] Man must act within his limited sphere, even though his action may ultimately prove futile — as Saint Nicolas sadly learned. The unforeseen consequences of one's acts make any action a gamble; and it is tempting to seek refuge in a suspension of action. The recluse, Jean, in *Le Jardin d'Epicure* declares: "Je ne cultive même pas mon jardin, de peur d'accomplir un acte dont je ne pourrais pas calculer les conséquences." [3] But his interlocutor, like

---

[1] France, "Sur le scepticisme," *La Vie Littéraire II*, VI, 451.
[2] France, "Sérénus," *La Vie Littéraire I*, VI, 24.
[3] France, *Epicure*, IX, 533.

Candide, warns him, "Quoi qu'on fasse, vivre c'est agir." [4] France's position is ironic yet fundamentally optimistic: "la résignation dans l'effort, qui consiste à frapper toujours le mal, sans nous irriter jamais de son invulnérable immortalité." [5]

This attitude involves a delicate balance. At times, the equilibrium is disturbed and France's world seems disproportionately bright or dreary — for example, in the bitter sarcasm of *L'Ile des Pingouins* or the sentimentality of his childhood memories in *Le Livre de mon ami*. But as a rule, France's pessimism is tempered with humor and pity and his sentimentality is balanced by self deprecation. France's irony is usually gentle; he construes laughter as an alternative to rancor:

> L'Ironie que j'invoque n'est pas cruelle. Elle ne raille ni l'amour ni la beauté. Elle est douce et bienveillante. Son rire calme la colère, et c'est elle qui nous enseigne à nous moquer des méchants et des sots, que nous pouvions, sans elle, avoir la faiblesse de haïr. [6]

Subjects for anger are never lacking. France abhorred any form of social extremism: the three "saints" venerated in his self-made Abbaye de Thélème were indulgence, tolerance, respect for oneself and others. [7] He found any form of intellectual absolutism absurd; first, because absolutes transcend experience and secondly, because such obdurate opinions reveal man as an unthinking automaton. France's comic universe is curved: any line of reasoning risks turning into a circular argument if it is pushed too far. Ironically, even skepticism is liable to this danger if it, too, becomes an *idée fixe* rather than a prudent approach to life.

---

[4] *Ibid.* The discussion ends with an existentialist rejection of suicide: it is defined as the most serious of actions, even though it leads to nonaction:

> —Il faudrait donc mourir pour être innocent et tranquille?
> —Prenez-y garde encore: mourir, c'est accomplir un acte d'une portée incalculable. (*Op. cit.*, 535.)

[5] France, *La Vie littéraire I*, VI, 299. Sareil has pointed out how this attitude anticipates Camus. The essential difference between France and Voltaire on the one hand, and Camus, is one of mood. See Sareil, *Anatole France et Voltaire*.

[6] France, *Epicure*, IX, 450.

[7] France, *La Vie littéraire* I, VI, 5.

Jacques Tournebroche is the first of France's characters to suggest the possibility that skepticism can lead to the rejection of experience and ultimately turn into gullibility:

> Je ne suis pas crédule, j'ai au contraire une propension merveilleuse au doute, et ce penchant me porte à me défier du sens commun et même de l'évidence comme du reste. A tout ce qu'on me rapporte d'étrange, je me dis: 'Pourquoi pas?' Ce 'pourquoi pas?' faisait tort, devant le ballon, à mon intelligence naturelle. Ce 'pourquoi pas?' m'inclinait à la crédulité, et il est intéressant de remarquer à cette occasion que: ne rien croire, c'est tout croire.[8]

Jacques wisely opts for moderation and common sense, concluding:

> il ne faut pas se tenir l'esprit trop libre et trop vacant, de peur qu'il ne s'y emmagasine d'aventure des denrées d'une forme et d'un poids extravagant, qui ne sauraient trouver place dans des esprits raisonnablement et médiocrement meublés de croyances.[9]

Ultimately, the skeptics may be right and the world may be no more than a web of illusions; but all too often illusions are simply the self-delusions of ignorance and sloth. Jacques' "why not" all too often becomes an automatic denial, and the result — automatic belief — is the same as an unthinking *parti pris*. Boillot has described France's humor as a satire of those people who:

> tourbillonnent dans un monde fantasmagorique d'illusions parce qu'ils répugnent à l'effort de la pensée, parce qu'ils s'en laissent imposer par la tyrannie des préjugés, des traditions, des habitudes, si bien que leurs jugements ne sont

---

[8] France, *La Rôtisserie de la reine Pédauque*, *Œuvres* (Paris: Calmann-Lévy, 1926), VIII, 133. Hereafter cited as *Rôtisserie*, VIII.

[9] *Ibid.* Cerf deliberately deletes the second part of his passage in order to distort France's position. Referring to Jacques, Cerf says, "He concludes that to believe nothing is to believe everything. Thus incredulity becomes credulity, skepticism becomes superstition, and France reduces his system to the absurd." (Cerf, *Anatole France*, pp. 125-126.) That is exactly the point that France is making.

plus des opérations indépendantes de leur esprit, mais de simples réflexes moraux que le milieu leur impose...."[10]

These are the people who populate *L'Histoire contemporaine*, *L'Ile des Pingouins*, and *Les Dieux ont soif;* but nowhere does France satirize this mentality more thoroughly than in "L'Histoire de la Duchesse de Cicogne et de M. de Boulingrin qui dormirent cent ans en compagnie de la Belle au Bois dormant."

As the title indicates, this story is not simply a retelling of the tale of the Sleeping Beauty. The priorities of the intrigue have obviously been shifted. The opening lines make this point clear: "L'histoire de la Belle-au-Bois-dormant est bien connue; on en a d'excellents récits en vers et en prose. Je n'entreprendrai pas de la conter de nouveau." (217) Instead of reinterpreting the well-known facts with a new twist, as he did in the stories of Bluebeard and Saint Nicolas, the narrator will use the original tale as the *point de départ* for a marginal intrigue culled from hitherto unedited "anecdotes relatives." The basic elements remain unchanged: a curse of death called down on the infant princess by a fairy who was not invited to her christening which is tempered by a kindlier fairy into a 100-year sleep. France's additions include the reasons for the omission of the wicked fairy and the steps taken by the royal household to avert or remedy the malediction. The action is focused, however, on the adventures of two lesser members of the court, as the title indicates: the Duchesse de Cicogne and Monsieur de Boulingrin.

This kind of "en marge" technique recalls Jules Lemaître's two volumes of stories, *En Marge des vieux livres,*[11] but the apparent similarity in approach is deceiving. There is practically no parody in Lemaître's sentimental stories. They continue in the same vein as the original, new shoots from the same root. On the contrary, France's stories in *Les Sept Femmes de la Barbe-Bleue* always create and capitalize on a contrast with the original tale.[12]

---

[10] Félix Boillot, *L'Humour d'Anatole France* (Paris, 1933), pp. 8-9.
[11] Published in 1905-1907.
[12] This contrast is essential in France's story. Balzac, for example, also retold the story of the Sleeping Beauty for his own philosophic ends in his "La Filandière," but although the tale is "dans le goût de Perrault" there is no attempt to contrast his version directly with the classic version.

If France found Pyrrho's skepticism lacking in subtlety, his own ideas on the subject are definitely complex. In his version of the Sleeping Beauty, he plays on skepticism's basic quandries: the limits of intelligence and experience in determining illusion and reality. At the same time, the story is a broadside attack against the nearsighted and narrow-minded "esprit de système" which typifies modern scientific thought at its worst.

The scientific method of research and scholarship promised to provide objective truths. It failed because both the perception and the selection of acceptable facts are arbitrary. The fundamental irony of the story lies in France's transformation of a generally defined illusion into a verifiable reality, which is denied because of his character's intransigent disbelief. Of course, his criticism can be extended to the "proven" truths of all systems belief — and is. France cannot resist drawing the obvious parallels with religion:

> Monsieur de La Rochecoupée ... respectait les croyances populaires, que tous les grands hommes d'État respectent. César était pontife maxime; Napoléon se fit sacrer par le Pape; M. de La Rochecoupée reconnaissait la puissance des fées. (225)

Christianity is included in the same category as paganism and superstition. The comparison of religion to fairy tales is pointedly reinforced by a humorous play on words: "il impatientiat souvent M. de La Rochecoupée par l'étalage d'un froid aféisme." [13] The sideswipe at religion is not so much an attack on Christianity, however, as part of France's general criticism of the religion of modern society — science.

The scientific method is based on the objective evaluation of data. But France points out that objective observation is next to impossible. Even in people's speech, habit contradicts fact. This

---

[13] France, XIX, 226. An earlier example of France's toying with the relationship of skepticism and credulity can be seen in the opinions of the unorthodox Abbé L***, who doubts everything except divine revelation and muses: "Ce serait même une question de savoir si la religion chrétienne n'a pas fourni au scepticisme de nouveaux arguments et si la foi ... n'a pas rendu la nature plus incompréhensible et la raison plus incertaine." (France, *La Vie littéraire* II, VI, 448).

is often the case in idiomatic expressions whose objective reality has disappeared. For example, after spindles have ceased to exist physically in the Sleeping Beauty's kingdom, they remain a linguistic entity: "On disait encore dans les campagnes: 'Le fuseau doit suivre le hoyau,' mais c'était par habitude, les fuseaux avaient couru." (224)

Prejudice is an even stronger form of mental laziness. It renders disinterested judgment impossible. The nature of the individual bias or obsession is irrelevant; all prejudices are equally destructive of objectivity, and eventually lead to folly. France's king, for example, is obsessed by etiquette:

> Ce malheureux monarque, plus encore que ses prédécesseurs, était esclave de l'étiquette. Son obstination à soumettre les plus grands intérêts et les devoirs les plus pressants aux moindres exigences d'un cérémonial suranné a plus d'une fois causé à la monarchie de graves dommages et fait courir au royaume de redoutables périls. (219)

King Cloche's reality is a system of prejudices which he justifies by an historical authority who is just as prejudiced:

> Madame de Maintenon a pu dire sans la moindre exagération qu' 'il n'y a point dans les couvents d'austérités pareilles à celles auxquelles l'étiquette de la Cour assujettit les grands.' Conformément au royal vouloir de son souverain, le duc des Hoisons, grand maître des cérémonies, s'était refusé à prier la fée Alcuine, à qui manquait un quartier de noblesse pour être admise à la Cour. Aux ministres d'État représentant qu'il était de la plus grande importance de ménager cette fée vindicative et puissante, dont on se faisait une ennemie dangereuse en l'excluant des fêtes, le roi avait répondu péremptoirement qu'il ne saurait l'inviter puisqu'elle n'était pas née. (219)

France plays on the sense of the word *née* to illustrate the king's distorted logic which contradicts the objective reality presented by the ministers. Because the fairy does not exist socially for the king she does not exist at all — she has not been "born." The sense of *née* shifts from a social sense of "well-born" to a more literal (and false) interpretation. Madame de Maintenon's dictum does not exaggerate only if the self-imposed restrictions of court and cloister are accepted as valid norms of conduct. Contrasted with an outlook of *Realpolitik,* the rigid behavior of both Madame de Maintenon and King Cloche is a gross exaggeration. But the weakness of the reasonable point of view can even be seen in France's choice of verbs: a participle for the ministers (représentant) opposed to an emphatic independant verb for the king (avait répondu péremptoirement). Cloche rejects the existence of this particular fairy in the same way that Boulingrin — the overly zealous skeptic — rejects the existence of the entire genus: because of an overweening sense of principle.

Boulingrin's rationalism renders his judgment as unreliable as the king's snobbery, but because of his supposedly objective basis his selective perception is all the more shocking. For France, it is simply another form of fanaticism:

> Ceux qui se demanderont comment il pouvait n'y pas croire puisqu'il les avait vues [les fées] ignorent jusqu'où peut aller le scepticisme dans un esprit raisonneur. (226)

Of course, any system of beliefs could be substituted for *scepticisme* and *raisonneur;* the obvious parallels are *superstition* or *religion* and *crédule.*

"Il n'y a rien d'odieux comme les sceptiques," says Cicogne. "Ce sont des impertinents qui se moquent de notre simplicité." (236) On the contrary, however, Boulingrin is shown to be the simpleton as his doubt is pushed to the limits of superstition. He criticizes the Prime Minister, Rochecoupée: "il manque de philosophie." His argument is clearly self-contradictory, offering a perfectly acceptable empirical basis for Rochecoupée's belief: "Il croit aux fées, sur le témoignage de ses sens." (230) The Prime Minister correctly points out that Boulingrin's *philosophie* is an obsession:

> Mais, en vérité, il y a des moments où je me demande, mon cher Boulingrin, qui de nous deux est le plus crédule à l'endroit des fées. Je n'y pense jamais et vous en parlez toujours. (226-27)

France offers no reassuring alternatives to these cogitative excesses. The more moderate characters are spared the ridicule of mechanical and rigid behavior but they, too, lose their dignity. Rochecoupée is presented as a practical man:

> Il n'était point sceptique; il n'était point incrédule. Il n'arguait pas de faux l'oracle des sept marraines. Mais, n'y pouvant rien, il ne s'en inquiétait point. C'était son caractère de ne pas se soucier des maux auxquels il ne savait rémédier. (225)

This practicality is for the most part the product of laziness, and Rochecoupée's judgment, although clear, is limited:

> Monsieur de La Rochecoupée avait les vues d'une homme d'État, et les hommes d'État ne voient jamais au delà du moment présent. Je parle des plus perspicaces et des plus pénétrants. (225)

Even the nominal representatives of science — "les personnes de savoir et de sens" — are shown to be ignorant or ineffectual. The queen appeals to her savants for practical help in avoiding the malediction, but intelligence, even when it is free from prejudice, provides no useful guide for action. M. Gerberoy, permanent secretary of the Academy of Sciences, supplies historical "facts" which are all drawn from myth and legend: Epimenidos of Cnossos, the seven sleepers of Epheses, Frederick Barbarossa, Brunhilda. History (and historical accuracy) are placed on the same level as nursery rhymes when Cicogne adds a few verses of the well-known song "Guenillon" to Gerberoy's examples.[14]

Dr. Gastinel, on the contrary, offers first-hand observations. Unfortunately, he is a genuine skeptic: he considers the empirical evidence but suspends final judgment:

> ... j'ai observé des cas curieux de léthargie que je puis, si elle le désire, porter à la connaissance de Votre Majesté ...

---

[14] It is worth noting that France was extremely familiar with the origins of the Sleeping Beauty tale and with parallel legends (see, e.g. the *Dialogue sur les contes de fées*) and could have provided Gerberoy with more erudite examples if he had wanted to make him seem more reputable. Gerberoy's long-winded enumeration resembles Pangloss' equally long-winded catalog of unfortunate kings in the conclusion of *Candide;* neither list is of any practical use.

> —Monsieur Gastinel, demanda le roi, la pointe d'un fuseau peut-elle causer une blessure qui fasse dormir cent ans?
>
> —Sire, ce n'est pas probable, répondit M. Gastinel, mais dans le domaine de la pathologie, nous ne pouvons jamais dire avec assurance: 'Cela sera, cela ne sera pas.' (222-23)

Thus in the rare instance when human judgment does not distort the facts, the facts are inconclusive.

More often, even if the witnesses are genuinely unbiased, the facts themselves are impossible to determine. Sensory input can be contradictory, as in the following exchange between Boulingrin and Cicogne:

> Comme il se frottait les yeux:
> —Boulingrin, lui dit sa belle amie, vous avez dormi.
> —Non pas, répondit-il, non pas, chère madame.
> Il était de bonne foi. Ayant dormi sans rêves, il ne s'apercevait pas qu'il avait dormi. (249)

Cicogne sees Boulingrin rubbing his eyes and surmises on the basis of this observation that he had fallen asleep; but Boulingrin, who has no sensory corroboration of having slept, does not find this information sufficient. Nor does Cicogne realize that she, too, has slept for a hundred years.

The problem of sensory perception is made even more difficult by France's ironic treatment of reality and illusion. He attacks the scientific method from two angles, both intelligence and experience. France tries to be more Pyrrhonian than Pyrrho. On the one hand, what is commonly considered illusion — the supernatural — is presented as fact. The implication is clearly that many accepted facts are in reality as illusory as fairy tales. This "reality" is then rejected by the skeptical Boulingrin. In the abstract, Boulingrin's disbelief is justifiable; but in the context of "real" fairies he is ridiculous.

France's technique is similar to that in the story of Bluebeard: traditional fairy tales, because they are familiar, give the impression of being fact, and indeed, within the context of the story they *are* fact.[15] The realistic treatment of the supernatural is in the French tradition — the French folktale's "goût du rationnel —[16] and thus France's realistic treatment is all the more plausible. This tendency is already well-established in Perrault's stories. His fairies are quite rational (they have been called Cartesian) even in their magic feats. Moreover, the explanation of the supernatural by a moral at the end of each tale removes Perrault's stories from the realm of the absolute fantastic.

But as in the story of Bluebeard, France carries this trend even further. He supplies concrete facts to the original fairy tale in order to create an impression of reality, that is, "real" fantasy. Perrault's princess is not named; in France's version she is christened Paule-Marie-Aurore. The princess' name is convincing because of its precision. Moreover, it gives an impression of family tradition since we "know" from Perrault's story that the princess' future children are named Aurore and Jour.[17] France's seven fairy god-mothers (anonymous in Perrault's story) are all well-known legendary figures:

> ...la reine Titania, la reine Mab, la sage Viviane, élevée par Merlin dans l'art des enchantements, Mélusine, dont Jean d'Arras écrivit l'histoire et qui devenait serpente tous les samedis... Urgèle, la blanche Anna de Bretagne et Morgue qui emmena Ogier le Danois dans le pays d'Avalon.[18]

Perrault's "beau Baptême" becomes an official state function, conducted by the "duc des Hoisons, grand maître de cérémonies." (218) Dates, names, titles — all sorts of details are specified in

---

[15] The major difference between the two stories is in the style of narration; the emphasis in the story of Bluebeard was the *way* in which Perrault's facts were presented. For a discussion of the concept of truth and falsehood in fiction see Todorov, *Le Conte fantastique*.

[16] Paul Delarue, *Le Conte populaire français* (Paris: Editions Erasme, 1957), I, 46.

[17] The princess is also named Aurora in the Tchaikovsky ballet, libretto by Marius Petipa and Ivan Vsevolojsky, which was first performed in St. Petersburg on January 15, 1890. The ballet was not performed in western Europe until 1921, and at any rate, the Russian librettists based their work on Perrault.

[18] France, XIX, 218. This enumeration is just as "real" as Gerberoy's list of historical precedents.

France's version of the story. Compare, for example, these passages from France and Perrault:

| France | Perrault |
|---|---|
| *Dix-sept ans, jour pour jour,* s'étaient écoulés depuis l'arrêt des fées. *La dauphine* était belle comme un astre. Le roi et la reine habitaient avec la Cour *la résidence agreste des Eaux-Perdues.* (231) | *Au bout de quinze ou seize ans,* le Roi et la Reine étant allés à *une de leurs Maisons de plaisance*...[19] |
| *Le roi Cloche,* averti que l'arrêt des fées était accompli, fit mettre la princesse endormie dans la *chambre bleue,* sur un lit *d'azur brodé d'argent.* (232) | Alors *le Roi,* qui était monté au bruit, se souvint de la prédiction des Fées, et jugeant bien qu'il fallait que cela arrivât, puisque les Fées l'avaient dit, fit mettre la Princesse dans *le plus bel appartement* du Palais, sur un *lit en broderie d'or et d'argent.*[20] |

The most striking technique of presenting fairy tale as fact (and the most obvious jibe at scientific realism) is direct quotation, complete with impressive parenthetical references. Footnotes automatically lend credibility, but when the footnoted material is simply a fairy tale the ironic intent is obvious. France quotes the 1895 Lefèvre edition of Perrault on three occasions — often enough to make his point without overdoing it. Perrault is accepted as a *bona fide* authority and no attempt is made to discredit him.

In several other instances France simply paraphrases Perrault without quoting him and without distorting his "facts." For example, compare the following passages:

| France | Perrault |
|---|---|
| Aurore se percera la main d'un fuseau; elle n'en mourra pas, | La Princesse se percera la main d'un fuseau; mais au lieu d'en |

---

[19] Perrault, pp. 98-99. Italics is this and the following citations are mine.

[20] Perrault, p. 99. France's silver and blue room may at first seem no more precise than Perrault's silver and gold, but the two metallic colors are a cliché binary pair which France disrupts.

| | |
|---|---|
| mais elle tombera dans un sommeil de cent ans dont le fils d'un roi viendra la réveiller. (220) | mourir, elle tombera seulement dans un profond sommeil qui durera cent ans, au bout desquels le fils d'un Roi viendra la réveiller. (98) |
| Le roi fit publier un édit par lequel il défendait à toutes personnes de filer au fuseau ni d'avoir des fuseaux chez soi sous peine de mort. (224) | Le Roi, pour tâcher d'éviter le malheur annoncé, défendait à toutes personnes de filer au fuseau, ni d'avoir des fuseaux chez soi, sur peine de la vie. (97) |
| Comme chacun prenait place à table, on vit entrer une vieille fée, nommée Alcuine, qu'on n'avait pas invitée. —Ne vous fâchez point, madame, lui dit le roi, de n'être point parmi les personnes à cette fête; on vous croyait enchantée ou morte. (218) | Mais comme chacun prenait sa place à table, on vit entrer une vieille Fée qu'on n'avait point priée parce qu'il y avait plus de cinquante ans qu'elle n'était sortie d'une Tour et qu'on la croyait morte, ou enchantée. (97) |

France's passages add no realistic details to Perrault's version. The effect here is simply to reinforce the atmosphere of *déjà lu*.

On the other hand, France occasionally eliminates details from Perrault's text for the sake of "realism," as in the following passages:

| France | Perrault |
|---|---|
| Or, à la nouvelle que l'arrêt des destins était accompli, la fée Viviane, marraine de la princesse, se rendit en grande hâte aux Eaux-Perdues. (235) | La Bonne Fée qui lui avait sauvé la vie, en la condamnant à dormir cent ans, était dans le Royaume de Mataquin, à douze mille lieues de là, lorsque l'accident arriva à la Princesse; mais elle en fut avertie en un instant par un petit Nain, qui avait des bottes de sept lieues (c'étaient des bottes avec lesquelles on faisait sept lieues d'une seule enjambée). La Fée partit aussitôt, et on la vit au bout d'une heure arriver dans un chariot tout de feu, traînée par des dragons (99-100) |

France has chosen to delete the more supernatural element—dwarf, dragons, flaming chariot and seven-league boots. He retains only the general idea of a hasty arrival. But in contrast, he identifies Perrault's anonymous "Bonne Fée" both by name and social role. And since the notion of Destiny is a fundamental concept underlying fairy tales — Perrault's king knew "qu'il fallait que cela arrivât, puisque les Fées l'avaient dit" — France reinforces the fairies' psychological authenticity by associating them directly with their classical grandmothers, the Fates: [21]

> La vieille Alcuine, enragée du mépris qu'elle essuyait, jeta à la princesse un don funeste. A quinze ans, belle comme le jour, cette royale enfant devait mourir d'une blessure fatale, causée par un fuseau, arme innocente aux mains des femmes mortelles, mais terrible quand les trois Sœurs filandières y tordent et enroulent le fil de nos destinées et les fibres de nos cœurs. (219-20)

Despite this surface realism, France's fairy-tale world is not entirely credible. The paradoxical reality he purports to establish — authentic fairy tale — is eroded at the same time it is authenticated. France adds verisimilitude with proper names, but not all of his names are "authentic" in fairy tale tradition. Bogus characters are scattered in with the genuine ones. King Cloche, Queen Satine and the fairy Alcuine are all unverifiable and hence unacceptable "facts." [22] This inconsistency, however, is of relatively little importance. It disrupts the fairy tale's "historical" authenticity but does not seriously threaten it.

There are far more serious consequences when France's realistic details threaten to cross the threshold between the real and the fantastic, that is, when he brings the fairies completely down-to-earth. When we say that fairies are "natural" in a supernatural context we do not mean to say that they are real; we are simply offering a new dimension of reality, one that remains opposed

---

[21] See e.g. Todorov, p. 116, or France's discussion of the etymology of the word fée in *Ami*, III, 138. Banville's sorceress in "Chez Brébant" is "une vieille, une fée, une parque." (Banville, *Contes Féeriques* [Paris, 1882], p. 273).

[22] Of course the whole notion of "verifiability" is absurd in the context of fiction, just as it is, for France, in histories.

to standard definitions of normalcy. The supernatural can either be accepted as the prevailing order of reality (as in the *merveilleux*) or co-exist with the natural world (as in the *étrange*) or be rejected as completely non-existant; but the supernatural cannot actually become natural, for that would be a contradiction in terms. Thus it is one thing for France's fairies to be real fairies, and quite another for them to be real. The reader, lulled by the many details substantiating the fairies' authenticity as fairies, is all the more surprised when they make the quantum jump into the natural world. The opposition between their fantastic and naturalistic qualities is exemplified by their apparel, which is simultaneously diaphanous and crystalline: "Elles parurent au château en robes couleur du temps, du soleil, de la lune et des nymphes, et tout étincelantes de diamants et de perles." (218)

Social relationships are the most characteristic attributes of human society, and the fairies are subject to the same social restrictions as mortals. Not all of them are invited to the christening as in Perrault's story, but in France's version the omission is based on social status rather than an oversight: only "celles qui étaient titrées" (218) are eligible. Alcuine, the oldest fairy, is not invited because, like the unlucky suitor in *Candide,* she lacks "un quartier de noblesse." (219) The fairy Mélusine's enchantment is treated like a social obligation which, luckily, can be fitted into her calendar: she "devenait serpente tous les samedis (mais le baptême se fit un dimanche)." (218)

As a disappointing anticlimax, the famous scene of the princess' awakening is portrayed in humorously prosaic terms. The reader is led to expect the "real," i.e. traditional scene:

> Chacun sait la fin de l'enchantement et comment, après cent cycles terrestres, un prince favorisé par les fées traversa le bois enchanté et pénétra jusqu'au lit où dormait la princesse. (239)

Previous appeals to such common knowledge have not been deceiving, as, for example, when the narrator asks:

> Qu'ai-je besoin de conter ce qui advint alors? On sait comment la princesse Aurore, courant un jour dans le château, alla jusqu'au faîte d'un donjon où dans un galetas, une bonne vieille, seulette, filait sa quenouille. (231)

France has even added "quaint" details to Perrault's text in this passage which reassure the reader of the fairy tale's authenticity: *faîte* rather than *haut; seulette* instead of *seul*.

But in France's version of the awakening, the reader is disenchanted as well as the princess. This is no "real" Prince Charming, an idealized composite of masculine attributes. On the contrary, this hero is ludicrous: "C'était un principicule allemand qui avait une jolie moustache et des hanches orbiculaires...." (239) France reaches the heights (or the depths) of literal interpretation when he describes the princess' reaction. In her reclining position Aurore cannot "fall" in love; thus, France explains, "elle tomba ou plutôt se leva amoureuse." (239) In the same way that fairies, who are creations of language, are reduced to every-day reality, France reduces the figurative cliché "tomber amoureuse" to its literal components. Another all-too realistic element in the scene is Aurore's ingratitude: she leaves without so much as a thank-you to all the people who shared her hundred-year sleep. This trait is recognized as a sign of Aurore's authenticity as a *bona fide* princess:

> Sa première dame d'honneur en fut touchée et s'écria avec admiration:
> —Je reconnais le sang de mes rois.[23]

Thus France's realism is unreliable, even when reality represents — paradoxically — fantasy. Moreover, despite this scene's amusing realism, it seems to fade into fantasy. The diminutives, the precipitous action (punctuated by a profusion of *p*'s) evoke Voltarian marionnettes:

> C'était un principicule allemand qui avait une jolie moustache et des hanches orbiculaires et dont, aussitôt réveillée, elle tomba ou plutôt se leva amoureuse et qu'elle suivit dans sa petite principauté avec une telle précipitation qu'elle n'adressa pas même une parole aux personnes de sa maison qui avaient dormi cent ans avec elle. (239)

---

[23] France, XIX, 239. France exaggerates an ironic realism that is already present in Perrault's version. His Princess' first words are rather impertinent: "Est-ce vous, mon Prince" lui dit-elle, vous vous êtes bien fait attendre." (Perrault, p. 102). The lovestruck couple do not notice that everyone else in the castle is dying of hunger; the impatient Dame d'honneur must interrupt them to announce dinner.

This ambivalence is basic to the structure of the story. Definitions of reality are precarious on all levels, natural and supernatural. Indeed, at the same time that the fairies are depicted with killing realism, the realities of human society are shown to be illusory. Like the fairy gowns, an outer shell of substance often masks an inner void. Appearances are patently false, particularly in social relationships.

For example, the courtiers must counterfeit concern for the princess:

> Agités et consternés les courtisans s'apprêtaient des larmes, essayaient des soupirs et se composaient une douleur. (232)

Paradoxically, this description of life at court is realistic since social reality *is* deceptive. France's choice of verbs emphasizes this deceit: the courtiers prepare their emotions as one would a costume *(s'apprêter, essayer)* or a role *(se composer)*. Similarly, Cicogne's attachment to Boulingrin is not based on genuine affection but corresponds to her social self-image:

> Elle avait des bontés por M. de Boulingrin et ne se refusait pas à un commerce auquel elle n'était point portée par tempérament mais qu'elle estimait convenable à son rang et utile à ses intérêts. (227)

What is more, social behavior is arbitrary when it is not deceitful. The baptismal ceremonies are conducted according to an illegible, hence senseless, set of rules, "un formulaire qui datait de l'empereur Honorius et où l'on ne pouvait rien déchiffrer tant il était moisi et rongé des rats." (218)

At the same time that the fairies become disquietingly real, France's human protagonists are turned into burlesque figures. Boulingrin is made "real" by details of local color. For example:

> La duchesse de Cicogne grimpa par le petit escalier chez son vieil ami, qu'elle trouva en bonnet de nuit, souriant, car il lisait *la Fiancée du roi de Garbe*. (232)

At the same time, however, he is a travesty of both myth and fairy tale. The epigram of Chapter II is taken from Catullus:

*Currite ducentes subtemina* [*sic*], *currite fusi.*[24] The song of the Fates and the image of running spindles is an appropriate commentary on the theme of destiny: the fairies have already been identified as the spinning sisters. But the Fates in Catullus' poem are singing about the life of the future hero, Achilles, and Boulingrin is far from an epic hero. His destiny is not noble; he and the duchess simply become hopelessly (and absurdly) entangled in the "threads of Fate." France does not insist on the contrast between Achilles and Boulingrin, but the implication is clear in his repetition of the Fate-fairy relationship after each of Boulingrin's grotesque adventures:

> Il passa sans avoir reconnu les fées, maîtresses des destinées. (228)

> Cette fois encore, M. de Boulingrin avait méconnu les fées, maîtresses des destinées. (229)

Boulingrin's encounters with the fairies are standard fairy tale intrigue;[25] and more specifically, his "reality" apes the tale of the Sleeping Beauty. While Aurore and her germanic princeling are humorous incarnations of the Sleeping Beauty and Prince Charming, Boulingrin and Cicogne are travesties of these characters. Boulingrin's adventures occur on the road to Cicogne's castle — not through a mysterious forest but through a humid swamp. One of the fairies makes the comparison explicit: "Mes sœurs, donnez congé à monsieur de Boulingrin, qui va-t-au château baiser sa belle." (228) And Cicogne completes the allusion by paraphrasing the princess' greeting (familiar to readers of Perrault but eliminated in France's realistic awakening scene): "Vous venez bien tard, mon ami." (229)

---

[24] Catullus, p. 64.
[25] "Les fées se présentent presque toujours sous l'aspect de vieilles femmes dans les contes populaires, et le héros qui les rencontre sans les connaître est récompensé ou puni selon la conduite qu'il observe à leur égard." (Delarue, *op. cit.*, p. 21n.) Think, e.g., of Perrault's *Les Fées*. The transformation from harpy to beautiful nymph and vice versa is also traditional. France's "Saint Satyr" is similar to Banville's "Chez Brabant" where the fairies, in both of their incarnations, seek the hero's love.

Boulingrin and Cicogne are surrounded by an even subtler aura of fairy tale. *Les Contes de la Cicogne* (cigogne = cicogne) are synonymous with the *Contes de ma Mère l'Oye*.[26] A *boulin* is a dovecote nest, and this ornithological undercurrent is reinforced by Boulingrin's summer residence — a *pigeonnier* — and the name of the *grand maître des cérémonies:* le duc des Hoisons (oison = oiselet).

Underneath all these bizarre undercurrents, however, France's basic paradigm remains: fantasy is real and this reality is rejected by science. The fairies attempt to make themselves real in scientific terms — to demonstrate their existence in an impromptu experiment in which Boulingrin is both the observer and the unwilling guinea pig. Their experiment cannot succeed because Boulingrin's prejudices interfere with an objective analysis of the empirical data.

Boulingrin's *Weltanschauung* does not admit the existence of fairies, therefore he will not recognize them even though he sees them undisguised and at close range. His parochial mentality is expressed by the use of his official title in the opening lines of his first encounter with the fairies: his concepts of what he is and what the world is insulate him from his experience:

> Or, un soir, tandis que les derniers reflets du soleil teignaient d'une couleur de sang les eaux croupies, le secrétaire d'État aux Finances vit, au carrefour du chemin, trois jeunes fées qui dansaient en rond et chantaient... (227)

Even though this reality is ambiguous (the scene takes place in the mysterious dusk of a blood-red sunset; the fairies' faces are blurred, their hair shimmers like will-o'-the-wisps), Boulingrin physically experiences this reality: he sees the fairies, hears their song and is dizzied by their dance:

---

[26] It is an interesting coincidence that Rabelais associates the story of Saint Nicolas with the fairy tales of La Cigogne: "Ce pendant Panurge leur contoit les fables de Turpin, les exemples de sainct Nicolas, et le conte de la ciguoinge." (Rabelais, II, 29.) Cited in Huguet, *Dictionnaire de la Langue Française du 16ᵉ Siècle*, II, 288.

> Elles l'enfermèrent dans leur ronde et agitèrent vivement autour de lui leurs formes minces et légères. Leurs visages, dans le crépuscule, étaient obscurs et limpides; leurs chevelures brillaient comme des feux follets.
> Elles répétèrent: Trois filles dedans un pré... tant que, étourdi, prêt à tomber, il demanda grâce. (228)

Boulingrin's second adventure is even more realistic than the first. The three fairies, now in the form of harpies, are described at length:

> Quelques pas plus loin il rencontra trois vieilles besacières qui marchaient toutes courbées sur leurs bâtons et ressemblaient de visage à trois pommes cuites dans les cendres. A travers leurs haillons passaient des os plus recouverts de crasse que de chair. Leurs pieds nus allongeaient démesurément des doigts décharnés, semblables aux osselets d'une queue de bœuf. (228)

Boulingrin's symbolic rejection of their love and the fairies' subsequent anger is depicted in detail. The immediacy and reality of these adventures are impressed on the reader by the transition in the narrative from the past tense (in the first encounter) to the present tense (in the second):

> Avec une longue frénésie elles le sollicitent à les aimer. Puis, voyant qu'elles ne parviennent point à ranimer ses sens glacés d'horreur, elles l'accablent d'invectives, le frappent à coups redoublés de leurs béquilles, le renversent à terre, le foulent aux pieds et, quand il est accablé, brisé, moulu, perclus de tous ses membres, la plus jeune... s'accroupit sur lui, se trousse et l'arrose d'un liquide infect. Il en est aux trois quarts suffoqué; et tout aussitôt les deux autres, remplaçant la première, inondent le malheureux gentilhomme d'une eau tout aussi puante. Enfin toutes trois s'éloignent en le saluant d'un "Bonsoir, mon Endymion! Au revoir, mon Adonis! Adieu, beau Narcisse!" et le laissent évanoui. [27]

The physical reality of this experience is emphasized by a series of actions of increasing physical intensity, both on the part of the

---

[27] *Ibid.* These ironic epithets conform with France's treatment of Boulingrin as a travesty of a classic hero.

harpies *(accabler d'invectives, frapper, renverser, fouler)* and on Boulingrin's part *(accablé, brisé, moulu, perclus)*. Boulingrin, who is on the receiving end of the action, is characterized by adjectives rather than the fairies' active verbs, but the rhymed and rythmic string of adjectives reinforces the action. The final indignity is repeated three times, to leave no doubt in Boulingrin's mind. But during the course of these harrowing experiences, Boulingrin's senses have tuned out: from *étourdi*, his senses become *glacés d'horreur* and he eventually faints, thus completely blocking his experience.

Both the realism of Boulingrin's encounters and the paradoxical relationship of reality and illusion in the story can be seen more clearly if this scene is compared to similar ones in "Saint Satyr"[28] and *Le Crime de Sylvestre Bonnard,* both written prior to "L'Histoire...." Boulingrin's encounters are an amalgam of the other two scenes, less horrifying than the first and less saccharine than the second. Boulingrin's experience lies completely within the parameters of reality which have been set up in the context of the story. The other scenes are clearly "abnormal" in context. In short, Boulingrin's experience is real, Sylvestre Bonnard's experience is unreal, and Fra Mino's experience is surreal.

Bonnard, like Boulingrin, is a skeptic. He does not rush to conclusions when he notices a tiny person seated on his copy of the *Chronique de Nurenberg.* Unlike Boulingrin, however, his definition of the creature's nature is based on an objective analysis of the facts. He studies her physical attributes, clothing, and accessories and makes a logical conclusion: "C'est, me dis-je, une baguette de fée; conséquemment, la dame qui la tient est une fée."[29] Having decided empirically that the creature is a fairy, he must then decide whether she is real. Even though he has sensory evidence of her existence (she has thrown nut shells at him and tickled his nose) he concludes, like Boulingrin, that she cannot be real because fairies do not exist. When the fairy objects, Bonnard's only reply is bewildered skepticism:

—Qu'en dites-vous? s'écria-t-elle d'une voix argentine...
—Je ne sais, lui répondis-je, en me frottant les yeux.

---

[28] In *Le Puits de Sainte Claire* (X).
[29] France, *Bonnard,* II, 356.

> Cette réponse, empreinte d'un scepticisme profondément scientifique, fit sur mon interlocutrice le plus déplorable effet.[30]

This second rejection invokes the fairy's wrath and she punishes Bonnard for his incredulity:

> Elle se tut; l'indignation gonflait ses fines narines et, tandis que j'admirais, malgré mon dépit, la colère héroïque de cette petite personne, elle promena ma plume dans l'encrier, comme un aviron dans un lac, et me la jeta au nez le bec en avant.[31]

The basic elements of this scene are the same as those in Boulingrin's encounters: double rejection of fairies and consequent punishment of the skeptic. But the entire interlude in *Sylvestre Bonnard* is characterized by incongruity: the fairy's regal yet childish behavior, her heroic anger expressed in silvery tones. Her very presence, perched on Bonnard's book, is incongruous, i.e., out of kilter with a concomitant standard of reality. The scene is, if you like, "real" fantasy. In "L'Histoire...," on the contrary, the existence of fairies has been established as the norm and Boulingrin is rejecting a real experience not a fantastic one. The difference in the fairies' physical stature in the two scenes is indicative of the difference in tone, and the escalation of intensity is obvious: tiny nutshells and spilled ink are replaced by a beating and a dousing with a much more noxious liquid.

Bonnard dismisses his experience as a dream and furnishes a rational explanation for his state of disorder:

> Un vent frais, qui s'était élevé sans que je m'en aperçusse, faisait voler plumes, papiers et pains à cacheter. Ma table était toute tachée d'encre. J'avais laissé la fenêtre entr'ouverte pendant l'orage. Quelle imprudence.[32]

---

[30] *Ibid.*, 358-59. Bonnard's "Je ne sais" is a parody of the humorous epitaph written for Pyrrho which France mentions in the *Vie littéraire* II: "En lisant ces mots, je songeai à l'épitaphe en forme de dialogue qu'un spirituel Grec de Byzance composa pour Pyrrhon. 'Es-tu mort, Pyrrhon? —Je ne sais.'" (France, VI, 449).

[31] *Ibid.*, 359.

[32] France, *Bonnard*, II, 356.

For Boulingrin, on the contrary, there is no reassuring standard of normalcy to contradict the reality of his experience. The "real world" he awakens to after his ordeal offers no explanations because it is the same equivocal world of his so-called illusion:

> Quand il reprit ses sens, un crapaud, près de lui, filait délicieusement des sons de flûte et une nuée de moustiques dansait devant la lune. (229)

In "Saint Satyr," on the other hand, France creates an authentically fantastic atmosphere in which the supernatural intrudes upon the natural world. Fra Mino, too, has an encounter with nymphs and harpies. Like Boulingrin, he is beaten and left lying in a stinking puddle when he rejects the hags:

> A cet appel, toutes, levant leur fouet épineux, châtièrent si rudement le malheureux fra Mino que son corps ne fut bientôt qu'une plaie. Elles s'arrêtaient par moments pour tousser et cracher et recommençaient ensuite de plus belle à jouer des verges. Elles ne cessèrent qu'à bout de forces.
> —J'espère, dit alors Néère, que la prochaine fois il ne me fera pas l'affront immérité dont je rougis encore. Laissons-lui la vie. Mais, s'il trahit le secret de nos yeux et de nos plaisirs, nous le ferons mourir. Au revoir, beau mignon!
> Ayant dit, la vieille s'accroupit sur le religieux et l'inonda d'une eau infecte. Chaque sœur à son tour en fit autant, puis elles regagnèrent l'une après l'autre le tombeau de saint Satyr, où elles entrèrent par une petite fente du couvercle, laissant leur victime étendue dans un ruisseau d'une insupportable puanteur.[33]

Boulingrin's experience seems mild in comparison with the monk's. The thorns, blood, and sadistic pleasure of the witches has been eliminated, for Boulingrin is essentially a comic character. But even though Fra Mino's encounter is more vivid than Boulingrin's, it is not as "real." The orgiastic nymphs and fauns he spies on are not "normal" in the context of a church crypt, just as

---

[33] France, *Le Puits de Sainte Claire*, Œuvres (Paris: Calmann-Lévy, 1926), X, 21. Hereafter cited as *Puits*, X.

Bonnard's fairy was not "normal" in the context of a library table. The subsequent transformation of the nymphs into hags (it is interesting that their transformation is not described in "L'Histoire...") and their disappearance into the tomb are all unnatural events. But unlike Bonnard, Mino cannot explain away this "dream" as fantasy; not, as in Boulingrin's case, because there was nothing unnatural about it, but because it was completely supernatural. Metaphor is not reduced to reality for Fra Mino; rather, reality is transformed into metaphor in a horrifying way. The monk's dream is a reality: the witches do substitute a sponge for his heart as a punishment, and his grotesque death is a drastic intrusion of the supernatural into the real world:

> Il se leva au petit jour, tourmenté de douleurs aiguës et dévoré d'une soif ardente. Il se traîna jusqu'au puits du cloître, où buvaient les colombes. Mais dès qu'il eut aspiré quelques gouttes d'eau qui remplissaient un creux de la margelle, il sentit son cœur se gonfler comme une éponge et murmurant: "Mon Dieu!" il mourut étouffé. [34]

In comparison, Boulingrin's adventure is realistic. Nonetheless, the reality of Boulingrin's experience has little impact on him. The fairies' demonstration has failed, as France explains, because:

> C'est le défaut de la méthode expérimentale, employée par ces dames, que l'expérience s'adresse aux sens, dont on peut toujours récuser le témoignage. (232)

And of course, in this context "experience" can be read as all of human experience, as well as the immediate experiment.

France's final lesson is that the reality represented by the fairies could never be apprehended by the senses. The supernatural is destroyed when it becomes natural, and the fairies ironically compromise themselves by stooping to the level of a scientific demonstration. The truth made explicit in *Sylvestre Bonnard* but only implied by omission in "L'Histoire...," is that the only true reality is the imagination. Bonnard's fairy posits the paradox:

---

[34] *Ibid.*, 40.

> Savoir n'est rien, imaginer est tout. Rien n'existe que ce qu'on imagine. Je suis imaginaire. C'est exister, cela, je pense! On me rêve et je parais! Tout n'est que rêve, et, puisque personne ne rêve de vous, Sylvestre Bonnard, c'est vous qui n'existez pas. [35]

For France, fairies represent "la beauté du monde,"[36] and if he were forced to choose, France would prefer to keep his illusions, certain that they reveal a more important human truth than scientific data:

> Pour ma part, s'il me fallait choisir entre la beauté et la vérité, je n'hésiterais pas non plus: c'est la beauté que je garderais, certain qu'elle porte en elle une vérité plus haute et plus profonde que la vérité même. J'oserai dire qu'il n'y a de vrai au monde que le beau. [37]

France imposes his ironic viewpoint on the reader by creating an atmosphere of constantly shifting standards of reality. These contrasts are dramatized by his frequent use of ironic juxtapositions. For example, King Cloche sacrifices "les plus grands intérêts et les devoirs les plus pressants aux moindres exigences d'un cérémonial suranné." (226) The opposing orders of politics and etiquette are intensified by the opposing superlatives. Or, France will juxtapose two concomitant and contradictory "truths." For example, the artificiality and false security of society is revealed by contrasting it directly with physical reality:

> La banqueroute, la hideuse banqueroute, était là menaçant de consumer les biens et l'honneur de la nation. La famine sévissait dans le royaume et des millions de malheureux mangeaient du plâtre au lieu de pain. Cette année-là, le bal de l'Opéra fut très brillant et les masques plus beaux que de coutume. [38]

---

[35] France, *Bonnard*, II, 359. Cf. *Le Dialogue sur les contes de fées:* "Les fées existent, cousine, puisque les hommes les ont faites. Tout ce qu'on imagine est réel: il n'y a même que cela qui soit réel." (*Ami*, III, 404).

[36] France, *Ami*, III, 436.

[37] France, *La Vie littéraire IV*, VII, 443.

[38] *Ibid.*, 226. Léon Blum calls France's ability to point out the contradictions of society the basis of his so-called "anarchism": "Ainsi les institutions actuelles sont absurdes, d'abord en ce qu'elles reposent sur des contradictions logiques, et surtout en ce qu'elles tendent à perpétuer les

The contrast is more complex than it might appear at first glance: the poor are forced to artifice out of necessity — eating plaster instead of bread — while the wealthy deliberately indulge in deception. In a similar contrast of social and material reality, Cicogne is simultaneously a *grande dame* and a pauper:

> femme de l'ambassadeur à Vienne, première dame de la Reine, qui appartenait à la plus haute aristocratie du royaume... et qui perdait au pharaon ses revenues, ses terres et sa chemise. (227)

France also uses juxtapositions to demonstrate the irrelevancy of scientific reasoning. Philosophy is contrasted with tradition in the following passage — with no discernable advantage for scientific precision:

> Une fois, deux fois, trois fois, cinquante, soixante, octante, nonante et cent fois Uranie referma l'anneau du Temps, et la Belle avec sa cour et Boulingrin auprès de la duchesse sur la banquette de l'antichambre dormaient encore.
> Soit qu'on regarde le temps comme un mode de la substance unique, soit qu'on le définisse une des formes du moi sentant ou un état abstrait de l'extériorité immédiate, soit qu'on en fasse purement une loi, un rapport résultant du processus des choses réelles, nous pouvons affirmer qu'un siècle est un certain espace de temps. (237-38)

Even the numerals are "unscientific" in the first, highly figurative sentence. Yet everyone knows that it simply means that the princess and her court slept for a hundred years. The technical language of the definition of time adds no greater understanding of the situation, mainly because (as with all scientific data) the theories are conflicting and hence inconclusive. France's conclusion, "nous pouvons affirmer qu'un siècle est un certain espace de temps," shows that such philosophical questions as the nature of time are irrelevant to practical functioning.

---

principes et les effets de la barbarie primitive au lieu de s'adapter à l'état présent des mœurs, aux besoins présents de la société. Et telle est, je crois, la formule juste du soi-disant anarchisme d'Anatole France." (Blum, "En Lisant," *Œuvres*, I, 88).

Thus common sense emerges as a positive value, a limited area of free action between the extremes of superstition and philosophical intransigency. The amusing exchanges between Boulingrin and Cicogne highlight this opposition between theory and practice. Cicogne's terse rejoinders contrast sharply with Boulingrin's rambling observations and his obliviousness to his situation. She counters talk about the senses with a vivid olfactory reaction and responds to doctrinaire stoicism with ready action:

> Il a le goût et l'intelligence des affaires; mais il manque de philosophie. Il croit aux fées, sur le témoignage de ses sens.
>   —Boulingrin, dit la duchesse, vous puez le pissat de chat. (230)
>
>   —La calomnie, dit Boulingrin, est le fléau du monde, elle a tué les plus grands hommes. Quiconque sert honnêtement son roi doit se résoudre à payer le tribut à ce monstre qui rampe et qui vole.
>   —Boulingrin, dit Cicogne, habillez-vous.
>   Et elle lui arracha son bonnet de nuit, qu'elle jeta dans la ruelle. (235)

Cicogne repeatedly points out reality to Boulingrin: "Boulingrin, lui dit sa belle amie, vous avez dormi" (240) and tries to persuade him that their adventure was not "normal." Her pragmatism is the only example in the story of the healthy common sense advocated by Jacques Tournebroche.

Nevertheless, the value of Cicogne's action is limited. She is no more able than Boulingrin to grasp the significance of the supernatural and attributes the mysterious events to a worldly "sombre intrigue." France's irony is directed at both of them; at the very moment both are rejecting the existence of fairies for their own reasons they are enchanted:

> —C'est possible, répondit le secrétaire d'État. Dans tous les cas, il n'y a pas la moindre féerie dans cette affaire. Les bonnes femmes de campagne peuvent seules croire encore à ces contes de Mélusine...
>   —Taisez-vous, Boulingrin, fit la duchesse. Il n'y a rien d'odieux comme les sceptiques. Ce sont des impertinents qui se moquent de notre simplicité. Je hais les esprits

"L'HISTOIRE DE LA DUCHESSE DE CICOGNE..." 105

> forts; je crois ce qu'il faut croire; mais je soupçonne ici une sombre intrigue...
> Au moment où Cicogne prononçait ces paroles, la fée Viviane les toucha tous les deux de sa baguette et les endormit comme les autres. (236)

When they awaken, both Boulingrin and Cicogne lapse into their habitual behavior:

> Cicogne jouait à la manille, la nuit, dans les cabarets, tous les sous qu'on lui avait jetés dans la journée et, pendant ce temps, Boulingrin, devant un saladier de vin chaud, expliquait aux buveurs qu'il est absurde de croire aux fées. (241)

The couple's greatest failing is a lack of imagination. It is not insignificant that Boulingrin slept without dreaming. Boulingrin's final observation is doubly ironic: "Rien n'est qui ne soit naturel." (241) Boulingrin denies the existence of the supernatural (which for France is the only reality) but as a tried and true skeptic he also considers the natural world an illusion. He is only briefly perturbed by the total transformation of society; his acceptance is as nochalant as his transfer from an ancient buggy to an express train:

> Boulingrin et Cicogne louèrent au régisseur du château une guimbarde du XVII$^e$ siècle, attelée d'un canasson déjà fort vieux quand il s'était endormi d'un sommeil séculaire, et se firent conduire à la gare des Eaux-Perdues, où ils prirent un train qui les mit en deux heures dans la capitale du royaume. (240)

This lack of curiosity is a generalized phenomenon: not only do Cicogne and Boulingrin lose interest in their surroundings, but they are equally ignored by others:

> Leur surprise était grande de tout ce qu'ils voyaient et de tout ce qu'ils entendaient. Mais, au bout d'un quart d'heure, ils eurent épuisé leur étonnement et rien ne les émerveilla plus. Eux-mêmes, ils n'intéressaient personne. On ne comprenait absolument rien à leur histoire; elle n'éveillait aucune curiosité, car notre esprit ne s'attache ni à ce qui est trop clair ni à ce qui est trop obscur pour lui. (240)

Thus the confines of human intelligence are ignorance and prejudice. Boulingrin and Cicogne are victims of illusion and prisoners of reality precisely because they lack the capacity to imagine a reality which transcends both the senses and the intelligence. For France, "Les dupes sont ceux qui ne voient devant eux rien de beau ni de grand." [39]

---

[39] France, *Ami*, III, 408.

CHAPTER IV

"LA CHEMISE"

The paradoxical tale of the shirt of the happy man is tailor-made for France's ironic wit. "La Chemise" is a negative fairy tale, the story of a magic talisman which does not exist. France uses the well-known parable of the shirt of the happy man to lay bare all of society's deceptions and illusions, leaving only a tedious and depressing reality in their place. It is the most philosophical of the stories in *Les Sept Femmes de la Barbe-Bleue* and it has been called the most pessimistic.[1] France does not satirize particular abuses of the scientific mentality in this story. Instead, he paints a general criticism of the spiritual bankruptcy of the modern ethos.[2] The story is thus less pointedly ironic but at the same time more generally devastating than any of the others.

The protagonist, King Christophe V, is a personification of the pessimistic attitudes France confided to his secretary, Jean-Jacques Brousson:

> Dans tout l'univers, la créature la plus malheureuse, c'est l'homme. On dit: "L'homme est le roi de la création." L'homme est le roi de la douleur, mon ami. Il n'est pas de preuve plus évidente de l'inexistence de Dieu que la

---

[1] See e.g. Jules Bois' review in *Les Annales* (4 juillet 1909), pp. 6-7.
[2] There are echoes of the specific criticisms of the preceeding stories, particularly of the obstinate empiricism depicted in "L'Histoire..." Quatrefeuilles, for example, "se défiait du raisonnement et n'en croyait, en toutes choses, que l'expérience...." (France, XIX, 281) And the king's renewed interest in Mme. de La Poule is so astonishing "qu'elle n'en pouvait croire le témoignage de ses sens et pensait rêver." (France, XIX, 256)

vie.... Ah! Si vous pouviez lire dans mon âme, vous seriez effrayé....

Il soupire: Il n'y a pas, dans l'univers, une créature aussi malheureuse que moi. On me croit heureux. Je ne l'ai jamais été une heure, un jour.[3]

But just as this emotional outburst was an exaggeration, "La Chemise" is a literary exaggeration. As one example of *bonheur manqué* follows another, the story becomes a travesty of pessimism, in much the same way that *Candide* is a parody of optimism.

France adopts the form and philosophical conceits of the eighteenth century *conte philosophique* for his tale, but his focus and conclusions are very much of the twentieth century. His emphasis on contemporary realism immediately sets the story apart from its eighteenth century predecessors. The oriental trappings which usually surround the narrative are abandoned. If "L'Histoire..." is a fairy-tale brought down to earth, "La Chemise" is a *conte oriental* made true-to-life.

The unidentified kingdom is like any modern European country — and tediously comparable to all of them. In a humorously extended analogy, France compares its capital to the major cities of Europe, insinuating that they are interchangeable:

> Ils allèrent dîner au parc royal, promenade élégante qui est à la capitale du roi Christophe ce qu'est le bois de Boulogne à Paris, la Chambre à Bruxelles, Hyde-Park à Londres, le Thier-garten à Berlin, le Prater à Vienne, le Prado à Madrid, les Cascines à Florence, le Pincio à Rome. (309)

Similarly (but without exaggeration) the local mountainous region is called "notre Savoie et notre Tyrol." (331) The imaginary country, city, and region are never named; only actual places are identified, thus weighting the comparisons on the side of reality. Many other details add to the contemporary realism of the story. The kingdom is equipped with all the benefits and drawbacks of

---

[3] Jean-Jacques Brousson, *Anatole France en pantoufles* (Paris: Editions G. Crès et C$^{ie}$, 1926), p. 61.

civilization: cablegrams and anarchists, factories and 200-foot yachts.

The monarch of this kingdom is also thoroughly modern. Unlike M. de Montragoux or Saint Nicolas, he is a shrewd and cynical judge of human nature. By all objective standards he is a successful king. But objective standards, so essential to modern science, are shown to be meaningless. Christophe has no illusions and he is dying of boredom. His power is unlimited but it brings him no satisfaction: his brief moments of happiness are found in an escape from reality:

> Il lui était fastidieux de fixer les destins des peuples; mais, ayant trouvé dans la cabine de madame de la Poule un vieux roman pour les petites ouvrières, il le lut avec un intérêt passionné qui, durant quelques heures, lui procura l'oubli délicieux des choses réelles. (257)

Such moments of escape are rare, however, and as a rule Christophe views reality with a jaundiced eye. He criticizes artists for idealizing nature:

> Ils prêtent une beauté touchante aux femmes qui pleurent et nous montrent des Andromaque, des Artemis, des Madeleine, des Héloise, parées de leurs larmes.... Et, dès que madame de la Poule commence à pleurer, sa face se convulse, son nez rougit: elle est laide à faire peur. (312)

Madame de la Poule is only too real for Christophe; she epitomizes all that is dull and uninteresting in life, and not even a Voltairian series of disguises can make her more appealing. She seems to embody the adage, "Plus ça change, plus c'est la même chose!"

> Parfois, excédé de ce qu'elle se montrât toujours fadement la même, il essayait de la varier par des déguisements et la faisait habiller en Tyrolienne, en Andalouse, en capucin, en capitaine de dragons, en religieuse, sans cesser un moment de la trouver insipide. (248)

France also modernizes the wizard or magician of the traditional versions of the story. Dr. Rodrigue retains the essential characteristics of a miracle-worker possessed of superhuman powers:

> A cette époque le docteur Rodrigue étonnait l'univers. On le voyait presque en même temps dans tous les pays du globe. (252)

Rodrigue's diagnosis is couched in a hocus-pocus of unintelligible scientific phrases, but his reputation is measured in capitalistic rather than cabalistic terms. His prices are a clear indication of his merit — to professionals as well as (and perhaps more than) laymen:

> Il faisait payer ses visites d'un prix tel que les milliardaires reconnaissaient sa valeur. Ses confrères du monde entier, quoi qu'ils pussent penser de son savoir et de son caractère, parlaient avec respect d'un homme qui avait porté à une hauteur inouïe jusque-là les honoraires des médecins... (252)

The implicit contrast between *honoraires* and a more disinterested possibility, *honneurs,* makes the physicians' materialism even more crass.

The contrasts in "La Chemise" are thus not between reality and illusion (mainly because this is a story of lost illusions) but between two mentalities, two fundamentally different ways of looking at reality: the faith in scientific progress and objective truths which characterized the philosophy of the Enlightenment, and the disillusioned view of the same philosophical current in retrospect. France does not contrast the "real" world with another order of existence. Instead, he simply shows that world for what it really is. In a sense, then, his text provides its own contrast. Furthermore, unlike the tales based on Perrault's stories, there is no single "authoritative" text which could provide specific parallels for the average reader. Even though France was probably familiar with Casti's "La Camicia dell'uomo felice"[4] he indicates both the popularity and the anonymity of the story by the source which he acknowledges in the epigraph: an excerpt from an

---

[4] See concluding Note.

illustrative anecdote in the "Grand Dictionnaire de Pierre Larousse, article chemise; t. IV, p. 5, col. 4." (243) The use of a dictionary reference rather than a fictional source is an ironic sidelight on one of the story's main themes — the futility of codification and definitions.

The basic form of "La Chemise" — the quest — is typical of the *conte philosophique*. In part, this form is a parody of the medieval romance. More importantly, however, it provides a framework for the classification and analysis of social classes and institutions. The object of the quest is less important than the insights revealed by the successive adventures of the hero. Thus Voltaire's *Zadig, Candide*, and *La Princesse de Babylone* all share the same basic plot — the search for an absent loved one — but romance is by no means the principal subject of the stories. In "La Chemise," the philosophical theme and the object of the quest coincide in the search for happiness. It is no accident that King Christophe's only passtime is hunting, for the *chasse au bonheur* was an obsessive theme in the eighteenth century.[5] Happiness was considered the only reason for living, and for the most part, happiness was believed to be within the reach of all, thanks to the "union de la philosophie, de la méthode des sciences exactes et de la littérature."[6] Philosophy provided the attitude, science the method, and literature the form for the diagnosis and cure of social and individual ills.

The generally optimistic attitude of the period is reflected in Voltaire's views on *ennui*. These comments occur, significantly, in his discussion of suicide — a passage which France utilizes in "La Chemise." In this instance, at least, Voltaire's cure was simple enough: "Le remède serait un peu d'exercice, de la musique, la

---

[5] "Au XVIIIe siècle, l'insistance à reprendre ce thème confine plus d'une fois à l'obsession. Le problème du bonheur est senti et proposé comme la clé de tous les autres, et l'on répète inlassablement avec Trublet: 'Tout se réduit au bonheur.... Rien n'importe que le bonheur; par conséquent rien n'importe que relativement au bonheur.' Le bonheur est le seul idéal concevable, la seule justification de l'existence humaine: aucune autre valeur ne se superpose à celle-là; toutes, au contraire, en découlent, et n'avoir pas su ou pu être heureux, c'est n'avoir rien fait de sa vie." (Robert Mauzi, *L'Idée du bonheur dans la littérature et la pensée françaises au XVIIIe siècle*, Paris: Armand-Colin, 1960, pp. 80-81).

[6] Mauzi, *Bonheur*, p. 256.

chasse, la comédie, une femme aimable." [7] None of these remedies is effective in Christophe V's case, however, and as a last resort he summons Dr. Rodrigue.

The idea of symptoms and cures for unhappiness was often taken quite literally in the eighteenth century. *Ennui (mélancolie, vapeurs)* was considered a genuine malady. King Christophe's nervous ailment corresponds to the eighteenth-century diagnosis of "l'irritabilité" or "racornissement" of the nervous system. [8] This illness was characterized by mental as well as physical symptoms. Christophe's complaints are thus completely authentic. He combines the physical and spiritual, the literal and the figurative in his description of his illness:

> J'ai constamment des verres noirs devant les yeux, et, sous les cartilages de mes côtes, je sens un rocher où s'assied la tristesse.
> Il perdait le sommeil et l'appétit. (249)

Conversely, the orator, Jeronimo, is assumed to be happy because he is so healthy: "Sa santé seule aurait dû assurer son bonheur; elle était solide et massive comme son âme." (273)

The cure proposed by France's Dr. Rodrigue bears a remarkable similarity to the materialistic theories of the "sympathistes" of the eighteenth century. [9] He gives a "scientific" rationale for the traditional remedy, the shirt of a happy man, explaining:

> Il ne s'agit donc plus que de se procurer en quantité suffisante des atomes de joie et de les introduire dans l'organisme par endosmose et aspiration cutanée. C'est pourquoi je vous prescris de porter la chemise d'un homme heureux... afin que votre cuir aride aspire les particules de bonheur que les glandes sudoripares de l'homme heureux auront exhalées par les canaux excréteurs de son derme prospère. (261)

---

[7] Voltaire, *Dictionnaire Philosophique II, Œuvres Complètes* (Paris: Garnier, 1878), XVIII, 90.

[8] Mauzi, "Les Maladies de l'âme au XVIIIe siècle", *Revue des Sciences humaines*, No. 100 (Oct.-Nov. 1960), 471.

[9] Rodrigue is thus doubly "materialistic".

The "sympathistes" explained the relationship between the emotional and the physical in terms of a "matière subtile qui se répand autour du corps et suscite des états d'âme nés d'invisibles et impalpables sensations." [10] Feelings of joy or hostility were thought to be absorbed through the skin: "cette matière sympathique n'est autre que ce que les médecins appellent la matière transpirante." [11]

Both the malady and the cure of France's hero conform to eighteenth-century thought, but the contemporary irony of France's attitude toward them is manifest in his text. His story demonstrates the breakdown of that "happy" union of philosophy, science and literature, as well as the individual inadequacies of each of the elements. Rather than take Christophe's ennui seriously, France relegates the human condition to the status of a minor physical complaint: "Enfin, hors quelques migraines, des névralgies, des rhumatismes et l'ennui de vivre, il se porta passablement." (258) The humorous juxtaposition of physical and moral terms is even more pronounced in Rodrigue's long monologue: *atomes de joie, derme prospère.*

In addition, the king's illness is parodied by the gallstone complaint of his *premier écuyer*, M. de Quatrefeuilles who laments: "Je sens à la vessie une chaleur et un poids qui me gâtent la joie de vivre." (267) France makes it clear that Quatrefeuilles suffers from a "philosopher's stone" — "sa pierre fondamentale, endroit par lequel il ressemblait à Montaigne." (267) The pun is quite apt: the promises of the philosopher's stone are as alluring and deceiving as those held out to Christophe V by Dr. Rodrigue. [12] And Rodrigue, the modern magician, not only reduces his "rational" prescription to absurdity; he also brings science full circle to superstition:

> Les médicaments que nous ne savons pas faire, il faut bien les prendre tout faits, comme les sangsues, le climat de la montagne, l'air de la mer, les eaux thermales natu-

---

[10] Mauzi, *Bonheur*, p. 313.
[11] *Ibid.*
[12] The source of this pun may well be Voltaire's *Dictionnaire Philosophique* (III): "Prétendre être toujours heureux est la pierre philosophale de l'âme; c'est beaucoup pour nous de n'être pas longtemps dans un état triste." (Voltaire, XIX, 344)

> relles, le lait d'ânesse, la peau de chat sauvage et les humeurs exsudées par un homme heureux... Ne savez-vous donc pas qu'une pomme-de-terre crue qu'on porte dans sa poche ôte les douleurs rhumatismales? (261)

"La Chemise" follows the traditional paradigm of the *conte philosophique*. In the course of their quest, the two seekers of the magical shirt, M. de Quatrefeuilles and M. de Saint-Sylvain, expose the ironies of life. Neither wealth nor fame nor success guarantee happiness. But within this pattern, France goes on to discuss and discard the major trends of eighteenth-century philosophical thought: the relative merits of luxury and simplicity, virtue and vice, reason and happiness; the golden mean, the pastoral ideal. At times, the satire is explicit, as in the following exchange:

> —Quatrefeuilles, mon ami, nous avons manqué de sens. Ce n'est pas à la cour ni chez les puissants de ce monde qu'il faut chercher un heureux.
>
> —Vous parlez comme un philosophe, riposta Quatrefeuilles; vous vous exprimez comme ce gueux de Jean-Jacques. (267)

Saint-Sylvain (his pastoral inclinations are indicated by his name) persists in his neo-Rousseauian ideals, and fails:

> Décidément, je crois à la vertu et je crois au bonheur. Ils sont inséparables. Ils sont rares; ils se cachent. Nous les découvrirons sous d'humbles toits au fond des campagnes....
>
> Quinze jours plus tard, ils avaient parcouru soixante villages de la montagne, sans rencontrer un homme heureux. (331)

France's irony is just as obvious in this exaggerated apology for wealth, studded with the vocabulary of the Enlightenment but contradicted by the acknowledged self-deception in the conclusion:

> Je vous parlerai des riches en *honnête homme* et en *bon citoyen*. Les riches sont dignes de vénération et d'amour;

> ils entretiennent l'État en s'enrichissant encore et, bienfaisants même sans le vouloir, ils nourrissent une multitude de personnes qui travaillent à la conservation et à l'accroissement de leurs biens. Oh! que la richesse privée est belle, digne, excellente! Comme elle doit être ménagée, allégée, privilégiée par le *sage législateur* et combien il est inique, perfide, déloyal, contraire aux *droits les plus sacrés,* aux intérêts les plus respectables et funeste aux finances publiques de grever l'opulence! C'est un *devoir social* de croire à la bonté des riches; il est doux aussi de croire à leur bonheur. (291-92; italics mine)

Several episodes in "La Chemise" are caricatures of eighteenth-century conceits. Le curé Miton is a perfect Vicaire savoyard — except that he has no faith; Jacques de Navicelle relates his amorous adventures in the guise of a *conte oriental;* and finally, Mousque, the happy man, is a grotesque version of the happy shepherd — a misshapen, simple-minded gnome.

France's criticism of the scientific method is even more destructive of the philosophical ideal. The *Encyclopédie* was the crowning achievement of the Enlightenment, a methodical analysis and explanation of the arts, the sciences, and the natural world. The enormity of the undertaking attests to the fundamental optimism of its editors. In contrast, the epigraph of "La Chemise" indicates France's constant preoccupation with the limitations of definitions. The first example is the king's illness. His doctors diagnose a nervous disorder. "Entité nosologique insuffisamment définie, par là même insaisissable." (250) The illness cannot be treated because it fits no recognizable definition. But, according to Dr. Rodrigue, even if it could be defined, this would in no way guarantee a cure:

> —Sire, dit-il, les médecins, qui parlent des maladies comme les aveugles des couleurs, disent que vous avez une neurasthénie ou faiblesse des nerfs. Mais, quand ils auront reconnu votre mal, ils n'en seront pas plus propres à le guérir... (254)

Rodrigue maintains that definitions are of little importance. Anyone, even the royal physicians, can devise one:

> Et d'abord, qu'est-ce que les nerfs? Si nous en demandons la définition, le moindre physiologiste, que dis-je? un Machellier, un Saumon nous la donnera. (260)

What matters, for Rodrigue, are natural essenses, inimitable and incomprehensible.

The concern with definitions is continued in the pursuit of Rodrigue's prescription: the shirt of a happy man. First, Quatrefeuilles and Saint-Sylvain debate whether the word "man" should be taken literally or generically and whether sex differentials alter the quality of happiness. Once this problem is resolved, Saint-Sylvain proposes a methodical approach to their quest: "Nous cherchons au hasard, sans méthode, nous ne savons pas au juste ce que nous cherchons. Nous n'avons pas défini le bonheur. Il faut le définir." (277) When Quatrefeuilles objects (he constantly opposes theory with common sense), his colleague persists and even defines what he means by definition:

> —Je vous demande pardon, répliqua Saint-Sylvain. Quand nous l'aurons défini, c'est-à-dire limité, déterminé, fixé en son lieu et en son temps, nous aurons plus de moyens de le trouver. (278)

Saint-Sylvain is seconded by the royal librarian, M. de Chaudesaigues, who contends:

> Le vague des mots produit le trouble de nos idées. Si nous prenions plus de soin de définir les termes au moyen desquels nous raisonnons nos idées seraient plus nettes et plus sûres. (282)

With the librarian's help, a definition of "happiness" — "etymologique et radicale" — is agreed on:

> Le "bonheur" ou "heur bon," c'est le bon augure, c'est le favorable présage tiré du vol et du chant des oiseaux, à l'opposé du "malheur" ou "mauvais heur" qui signifie un essai infortuné des volailles, le mot l'indique. (282)

This good fortune can be recognized by certain "signes extérieurs et visibles": a happy man is "un homme chanceux, c'est-à-dire un homme pour qui les oiseaux n'aient que de bons présages et que les dés favorisent constamment." (283)

These outward manifestations recall France's passing definition of a hunchback: "un tout petit homme, apparemment bossu, car on lui voyait le dos par-dessus la tête...." (266) The significantly placed detail — *apparemment* — is disturbing, for it signals the fundamental arbitrariness of language. The man is "apparently" hunchbacked because the word hunchback is an arbitrary definition of his condition. He is a hunchback because he has a hump. But etymologies are not essences, and knowing what happiness means is not the same thing as knowing what it means to be happy.

The definition of happiness, then, like the definition of Christophe's illness, is of little practical use. It is simply one more of the "généralités transcendantes qui passent par-dessus les têtes et n'embrassent personne." (269) Happiness thus defined is a null set since only those on the threshold of death can be called truly "happy." Everyone else is subject to the caprices of fortune. A happy young husband learns that his family has been killed in a freak accident; even the heroic duc de Volmar loses out on "sa dernière partie de dés. "(290) By definition, absolute happiness is unobtainable. The absurdity of this definition is illustrated by the suicide of the handsome young man who completely satisfies all the requirements for happiness:

> l'héritier d'une famille noble et riche, aussi intelligent que beau et constamment favorisé par le sort. [13]

---

[13] France, XIX, 317. Levaillant points out that this episode is based on the description of Philippe de Mordaunt in Voltaire's *Dictionnaire philosophique* (article "De Caton — du suicide"). In this passage, however, Voltaire is not concerned with a definition of happiness. He uses the example to ridicule suicide: "Tel homme qui dans un excès de mélancolie se tue aujourd'hui aimerait à vivre s'il attendait huit jours." (Voltaire, XVIII, 90). It is interesting, however, that in Voltaire's opinion as well as France's Mordaunt is ridiculous because of overly principled behavior: "Il se conduisit selon ses principes et se dépêcha d'un coup de pistolet...." (p. 92) Levaillant sees a serious argument for suicide on France's part in this passage. It is certainly sublime, but there are equally passionate arguments for life elsewhere in the story, e.g. the atheist Larive-du-Mont's monologue, p. 306.

Only his death can confirm his good fortune. This kind of happiness is not human; indeed, the young man's decision to commit suicide makes him godlike: "Je possède un bonheur absolu et me confonds avec la divinité." (316)

This paradoxical happiness is the result of a definition pushed beyond reasonable limits. It can be compared with the unhappiness of two other characters which is also caused by philosophical intransigency. La Galissonnière and Larive-du-Mont are miserable only because they "forcent trop violemment leur doctrine à les rendre misérables." (307) The most extreme example of such overreaction is the anecdote of a financier "qui, de peur d'être atteint par la contagion et ne connaissant pas de retraite assez sûre, se suicida." (302)

What is more, no objective measure of happiness can be applied as long as people judge their situation subjectively. Selective perception is a recurring theme in "La Chemise." It is most dramatically illustrated in the following exchange between Quatrefeuilles (the realist) and the prince de Lusance:

>—Ce tuyau! ... murmura-t-il d'une voix altérée, en désignant du doigt une cheminée d'usine qui fumait à plus d'une demi-lieue du parc.
>—Cette cheminée? On ne la voit guère, dit Quatrefeuilles.
>—Je ne vois qu'elle, répondit le prince. Elle me gâte toute cette vue, elle me gâte la nature entière, elle me gâte la vie. (296-97)

This kind of subjectivity is all too common among France's characters. The wealthy baron Nichol "se croit ruiné et se lamente nuit et jour." (299) M. Brome transforms the most insignificant facts into portents of imminent social revolution and, "se croyant toujours à la veille d'une catastrophe universelle, il vivait dans un perpétuel effroi." (308) The relativity of what is important and what is insignificant can also be seen in the banal query of the marquis de Granthosme which, to him, is "d'une extrême importance." Quatrefeuilles dismisses these "maux imaginaires" as less significant than physical "maux réels," but France allows no comfort from illusions in "La Chemise." As Saint-Sylvain points out, "Tous les maux sont réels dès qu'on les éprouve, et le rêve de la douleur est une douleur véritable." (302) The sad case of

Mme. de la Poule seems to corroborate Saint-Sylvain's theory. She, too, suffers delusions:

> Au contact du roi, madame de la Poule, devenue mélancolique, nourrissait des idées sombres et de folles terreurs. Elle se croyait persécutée, victime de machinations abominables; elle vivait dans la crainte perpétuelle d'être empoisonnée et obligeait ses femmes de chambre à goûter tous les plats de sa table. (312)

The reality confirming her paranoid fears becomes obvious in her last, brief appearance, where she exhibits genuine symptoms of poisoning:

> A peine habillé, Christophe V enjamba madame de la Poule qui se tordait à terre dans des convulsions, dégringola les escaliers et traversa le jardin à la course. (314)

These personal interpretations of happiness clearly inhibit objective and orderly analysis. Moreover, the supposedly exact sciences and objective disciplines are shown to be equally disorderly and subjective. The Royal Library is a modern tower of Babel, whose books

> disputent de tout: Dieu, la nature, l'homme, le temps, le nombre et l'espace, le connaissable et l'inconnaissable, le bien, le mal; ils examinent tout, contestent tout, affirment tout, nient tout. Ils raisonnent et déraisonnent. (279)

France forces the reader to participate in his play on definitions. He does not name specific areas of intellectual endeavor, but provides a definition — critical but clearly recognizable. The reader must supply the appropriate label. Thus metaphysical works are rejected as:

> une espèce austère et morne qui ne spéculent que sur des objets dépouillés de toute qualité sensible et mis soigneusement à l'abri des contingences naturelles; ils se débattent dans le vide et s'agitent dans les invisibles catégories du néant, et ceux-là sont d'acharnés disputeurs qui mettent à soutenir leurs entités et leurs symboles une fureur sanguinaire. (280)

Similarly, history books are completely dismissed: "Je ne m'arrête pas à ceux qui font des histoires sur leur temps ou les temps antérieurs, car personne ne les croit." (280)

All systematic endeavor in the story proves to be either fraudulent or unsuccessful. The precision of military strategy, for example, where battle orders are neatly indicated on maps with little squares and miniature flags, is simply glorified hindsight: "c'est le génie des grands capitaines d'ériger en système, à leur gloire, les caprices du hasard." (288) The duc de Volmar's serendipitous victory is an ironic example of this procedure. Chaudesaigues insists that "le duc de Volmar a toujours tout prévu." But he contradicts himself in his account of the battle:

> Il opérait sa retraite quand il apprit que les ennemis, en pleine déroute, se précipitaient éperdument dans le Danube. Aussitôt il fit volte-face, se jeta à leur poursuite et acheva leur destruction. (288)

The only exact science is, ironically, the most derivative and the most useless: cataloging. And the price of this comforting precision is ignorance. Froidefond seems tranquil and happy "pour n'avoir jamais pénétré au dedans d'un livre." [14] The entire intellectual process fares badly in "La Chemise," and Quatrefeuilles pleads — after a stunning argument in which vice is defined as virtue and vice versa — "Messieurs... ne raisonnons donc point. Nous ne sommes pas faits pour cela." [15]

After the failure of the official "commission du bonheur," Quatrefeuilles and Saint-Sylvain are ready to admit the uselessness of the scientific method:

> Je voulais procéder avec une méthode exacte et rigoureuse; j'avais tort. La science nous égare. Revenons au sens commun. On ne se gouverne bien que par l'empirisme le plus grossier. Cherchons le bonheur sans vouloir le définir. (290)

---

[14] France, XIX, 281. Froidefond's ignorance is an illustration of France's definition in *Le Jardin d'Epicure:* "L'ignorance est la condition nécessaire, je ne dis pas du bonheur, mais de l'existence même. Si nous savions tout, nous ne pourrions supporter la vie une heure." (France, IX, 409)

[15] *Ibid.*, 328, cf. in *L'Anneau d'Améthyste*: "Le mensonge est le principe de toute vertu et de toute beauté chez les hommes." (France, XII, 123)

Unfortunately, however, not even vulgar empiricism is much help in the search for happiness. Quatrefeuilles' "practical" approach is comically inefficient: "On ne doit jamais se mettre en campagne sans cartes! dit-il. Mais le diable, c'est de les lire." (291) His pragmatism can be summed up by the tautology: "C'est parmi les heureux qu'il faut chercher un heureux." (291) The happy do, indeed, possess happiness — but the commodity is definitely non-transferable. France's happy man is, significantly, one who has never devoted any thought to happiness: "Mousque ne put répondre, faute d'avoir réfléchi sur le bonheur." (340) Mousque is a caricature, but he also represents a compromise between the ignorant bliss of a Froidefond: "ce n'est pas vivre que d'ignorer qu'on vit; ce n'est pas être heureux que d'ignorer qu'on l'est" (281) and the wretched genius of a Larive-du-Mont: "De quel prix se paie la pensée! Vous êtes malheureux, mon ami, parce que votre pensée est plus vaste et plus forte que celle des animaux et de la plupart des hommes. Et je suis plus malheureux que vous parce que j'ai plus de génie." (307)

The search for happiness is doomed to failure from the beginning. It is a farce, both literally and stylistically. From the first sentence — "Christophe V n'était pas un mauvais roi" — to the last — "Il n'avait pas de chemise" — the use of negative constructions in "La Chemise" is striking. King Christophe V is guided by the theory of negative and contradictory action we have seen at work in the tales of Bluebeard and Saint Nicolas:

> Christophe V avait remarqué que ses actes ou ne produisaient pas d'effet appréciable ou produisaient des effets contraires à ceux qu'il en attendait. Aussi agissait-il peu. (247)

This theory is illustrated throughout the story by the experiences of the king and other characters. Numerous contradictions prepare and reflect the story's final paradox. One character, for example, becomes more secretive the more he confides:

> Jacques de Navicelle causait volontiers, se montrait ouvert et naturel; il faisait même des confidences, mais elles enveloppaient son secret et le rendaient plus impénétrable. (310)

Or, in another instance, the King points out the paradoxical relationship of "official" and actual reality. He observes that all his kingdom's nightspots are still open despite the fact that they had all been closed: "Mon préfet de police a fait fermer tous les claquedents: n'en sont-ils pas moins ouverts?" (313)

The reader, too, participates in this game of frustrated expectations when Christophe complains about his investigators:

> Vous me laisserez mourir, comme font mes médecins Machellier et Saumon. Mais, eux, c'est leur métier. (313)

After the qualifying "mais" we expect the king to justify his doctors instead of attacking them.

In the opening pages of the story, even before the king's theory is expounded, a curious system of negative logic is evident. Christophe is not a good king; he is, rather, not a bad king. He acquiesces in order to rule and appoints revolutionaries in order to insure order:

> Christophe V n'était pas un mauvais roi. Il observait exactement les règles du gouvernement parlementaire et ne résistait jamais aux volontés des Chambres. Cette soumission ne lui coûtait pas beaucoup, car il s'était aperçu que, s'il y a plusieurs moyens d'arriver au pouvoir, il n'y en a pas deux de s'y maintenir ni deux façons de s'y comporter, que ses ministres, quels que fussent leur origine, leurs principes, leurs idées, leurs sentiments, gouvernaient tous d'une seule et même façon et que, en dépit de certaines divergences de pure forme, ils se répétaient les uns les autres avec une exactitude rassurante. Aussi portait-il sans hésitation aux affaires tous ceux que les Chambres lui désignaient, préférant toutefois les révolutionnaires comme plus ardents à imposer leur autorité. (246)

This political strategy (which is perfectly logical, as the "aussi" indicates) is reiterated *à propos* of the powerful opposition legislator, Jeronimo: "Il ne doit pas souhaiter de changement, puisqu'il est de l'opposition." (275) Again, the logic of the argument is indicated by the subordinating conjunction *puisque* but is undermined by the contradictory meaning which is expressed. The king's popularity is based on negative esteem:

> Il n'était ni très aimé ni très estimé de son peuple ce qui lui assurait l'avantage précieux de ne jamais donner de déceptions. Exempt de l'amour public, il n'était point menacé de l'impopularité assurée à quiconque est populaire. (246)

In a similar manner, he supports the Church by not opposing it:

> Le roi Christophe protégeait la religion. A vrai dire, il n'était pas dévot, et, pour ne point penser contrairement à la foi, il prenait l'utile précaution de n'en examiner jamais aucun article. Il entendait la messe dans sa chapelle et n'avait que des égards et des faveurs pour ses évêques, parmi lesquels se trouvaient trois ou quatre ultramontains qui l'abreuvaient d'outrages. (247)

Even his positive benevolence toward his bishops is couched in negative terms *(ne... que)* and the reaction to his *faveurs* and *égards* is the opposite of what one would expect *(outrages)*. Finally, Christophe's success is measured by the absence of serious disturbances during his reign, and his reaction to this success is typically negative:

> Après dix ans d'un règne sans révolutions ni guerres, tenu enfin par ses sujets pour un habile politique, érigé en arbitre des rois, Christophe V ne goûtait nulle joie au monde. (249)

The king's illness is also developed in negative and paradoxical terms. At first, it is treated by neglect:

> Au début, la maladie du roi ne leur causait pas d'inquiétude. Ils comptaient que le malade en guérirait pendant qu'ils le soigneraient et que cette coïncidence serait notée à leur avantage.[16]

When the malady persists, it is diagnosed as a sympathetic pain, and therefore, a non-existent illness: "Ni l'estomac, Sire, ni l'in-

---

[16] France, XIX, 251, cf. Rabelais: "Ne sçais-tu qu'on dict, en proverbe commun, heureux estre le medecin qui est appelé sur la déclination de la maladie? La maladie de soy criticquoit et tendoit à fin, encores que le medecin n'y survint." (III, xli) *Œuvres completes* (Paris: Garnier frères, 1962), I, 575.

testin de Votre Majesté n'est malade...." (252) The king's condition does not improve when he contradicts his doctors' orders, but when he follows their advice he becomes even sicker:

> A la suite de cette abstinence et de ces soins, il fut saisi d'un tel accès de suffocation que la langue lui sortait de la bouche et les yeux de la tête. (256)

Frustrated expectations are at the core of the structure of "La Chemise." The negative attitude developed in the opening chapters is reinforced by one example of unhappiness after another. France reveals the fears, hopes, ambitions and jealousies which impede lasting felicity. "Je n'ai vue que des heureux," says Quatrefeuilles, "et leur bonheur à tous était gâté." (276) The story progresses through a series of checks and balances rather than a progressive linear development. Each potentially happy individual is frozen into a state of frustrated equilibrium, either because of his own internal contradictions or in contrast with another character.

The main theme of "La Chemise" is not so much that happiness is impossible but that man irrationally creates his own unhappiness:

> Les hommes ont pour souffrir des motifs contraires et des raisons opposées. [17]

Contrasts and oppositions thus form the basic structure of the story, culminating in the final paradox which is presented in terms of a verbal opposition: Mousque, the woodsman, is happy: "il répondit qu'il *l'avait* [le bonheur]" but he has no shirt: "il *n'avait pas* de chemise." (343; italics mine) France maintains interest in the story by varying both the tempo and the structure of these contrasts. Cursory generalizations are balanced by lengthier, detailed examples.

Two characters frequently cancel one another. A single phenomenon provokes two diametrically opposed reactions, both of

---

[17] France, XIX, 277. France repeats this theme: "Cette fois encore Saint-Sylvain observa que bien souvent les hommes s'affligent pour des raisons opposées et contraires." (p. 302)

which are motives for unhappiness. In the case of M. Brome and M. Sandrique, for example, "C'est de l'état public que tous deux tiraient la cause de leur souci; mais ils la tiraient à rebours." (303) The fear of death makes both M. Galissonnière and M. Larive-du-Mont miserable; one, because he is an atheist and regrets losing life, the other, because he is religious and fears Divine justice. Religion is the source of misery for two more characters. The wise and benevolent curé Miton weeps because he has no faith, and the town idiot, Hurtepoix, is reduced to tears because of his innocent belief in Christ. The royal physicians, Saumon and Machellier, form another contrasting pair. They are opposites in physical appearance and personality but united in their mutual opposition:

> Ils se haïssaient; mais, s'étant aperçus qu'en se combattant *l'un l'autre* ils se détruisaient *tous deux*, ils affectaient *une entente parfaite* et *une communion plénière* de pensées.... (251; italics mine)

The pattern of contrast and opposition is repeated on a more detailed level throughout the story. Even the names of characters are in opposition, as in the case of the two royal librarians, Chaudesaigues and Froidefond. France's frequent use of oxymorons in "La Chemise" is striking: *injustice justice, bonheur désespéré, déférence insolente, pompeux abaissement, charmante ovariotomie.* Such verbal gymnastics demonstrate the complexities of real life, where logical incongruities abound. This pragmatism explains why Christophe V awards medals to his enemies, thus leaving them "avilis et satisfaits" (247): an incongruous action leads to equally paradoxical results. The grim realities of Fortune's game of chance are described in similarly contradictory terms: Destiny's dice are "glorieusement pipés." (284) The nouveau-riche imposture of the wealthy industrialist Feligne-Cobur is expressed by his modern medieval castle, a "château tout neuf" equipped with "tours crénelées" and "murs percés de mâchicoulis, hérissés d'échauguettes." (294) One of the most direct oppositions in the text is simply a variation on an old joke. When his illness is characterized as "une douleur sympathique" the king retorts: "Je la trouve antipathique." (251)

Mutually exclusive terms are used to describe professor Quilleboeuf's exclusive audience — "à la fois une foule et une élite." (319) Aside from the obvious opposition of *foule* and *élite*, this contrast also reinforces France's concern with definitions, since the existence of any entity thus defined is a logical impossibility. One of France's most elaborately developed oppositions is also an example of an ironic definition:

> Sur les trois marches tendues de pourpre, une troupe de femmes couchées, magnifiques ou charmantes, longues, minces et serpentines, ou rondes, drues, d'une splendeur massive, toutes également belles de désir et d'amour, ardentes et pâmées, se tordaient à ses pieds. Dans tout le hall, une foule frémissante de jeunes Américaines, de financiers israélites, de diplomates, de danseuses, de cantatrices, de prêtres catholiques, anglicans et bouddhistes, de princes noirs, d'accordeurs de pianos, de reporters, de poètes lyriques, d'impresarii, de photographes, d'hommes habillés en femmes et de femmes habillées en hommes, pressés, confondus, amalgamés, ne formaient qu'une seule masse adorante, au-dessus de laquelle, grimpées aux colonnes, à cheval sur les candélabres, pendues aux lustres, s'agitaient de jeunes et agiles dévotions. Ce peuple immense nageait dans l'ivresse : c'était ce qu'on appelait une matinée intime. (321)

France builds up to the final ironic opposition *peuple immense/matinée intime* through a series of balanced contrasts: *longues, minces et serpentines/rondes, drues, d'une splendeur massive; ardentes/pâmées; hommes habillés en femmes/femmes habillées en hommes*. At the same time, the contrasts are not overbearing since they are included among such a bizarre agglomeration of characters.

Contrasts and oppositions are also found in descriptions of individuals. This technique is exemplified by the king's bizarre sensations: "Il endurait l'horrible supplice d'un homme pris dans les glaces depuis les pieds jusqu'à la ceinture et le buste enveloppé de flammes." (258) For example, the composer, Sigismond Dux, is a combination of opposites both in appearance — "grand comme le monde et mignon comme un amour"; "il montrait dans sa barbe grise des dents de jeune enfant" (320) — and temperament: "le plus spiritualiste et le plus sensuel des génies, heureux comme un dieu, tranquille comme une bête, joignant dans ses innombrables amours à la délicatesse la plus exquise le cynisme le plus brutal." (320) Jeronimo, the political leader, owes his position to his skill in reconciling contradictions: "il était devenu chef de l'opposition sans se brouiller avec le pouvoir et, travaillant dans le peuple, fréquentait l'aristocratie." (273)

Behavior as well as personality takes on patterns of contrast. Christophe V reverses all his doctors' orders:

> Non seulement il ne fit plus rien de ce qu'ils lui ordonnaient, mais encore il prit grand soin d'observer au rebours leurs prescriptions: il demeurait étendu quand ils lui recommandaient l'exercice, s'agitait quand ils lui ordonnaient le repos, mangeait quand ils le mettaient à la diète, jeûnait quand ils préconisaient la suralimentation; et montrait à madame de la Poule une ardeur si inusitée qu'elle n'en pouvait croire le témoignage de ses sens et pensait rêver. (256)

Manifesting a similar contrariness, the duc de Volmar "a tour à tour défendu et combattu toutes les nations d'Europe...." (285)

More important than this vascillating behavior, however, are the transformations of personality which form an essential mechanism of the story. France's most elaborately prepared transformation is found in the duc de Volmar. The notion of his physical grandeur is first introduced by association with his extensive exploits; his campaign maps stretch out "à perte de vue." His moral superiority is described in terms of physical stature. As Quatrefeuilles and Saint-Sylvain contemplate an equestrian statue of the general, the courtisan murmurs (in ironically literal terms): "Cet homme est grand de cent coudées." (289) Volmar's description is couched in terms of elegance and decorum, and the aggrandizement is extended to his lifespan: "Chargée de gloire et d'honneurs, il prolonge au delà du terme ordinaire, dans la richesse et la paix, son auguste vieillesse." (288) Most of all, the "sauveur de sa patrie" is presented as a proud man. His "fières paroles" are inscribed in Latin on the base of his statue and on the commemorative medal which celebrates his victories. The sudden appearance of the duke shatters this image. We see, if you will, **the flip side of the medal:**

> Soudain, les battants brusquement écartés, un très petit vieillard, lancé à coups de pied par une robuste servante, s'abattit comme un mannequin sur les marches, dégringola l'escalier, la tête la première, et tomba cassé, disloqué, brisé, dans le vestibule, devant les valets solennels. C'était le duc de Volmar. (289-90)

The new description *(un très petit vieillard, mannequin, dégringola)* is in opposition not only with the previous images of Volmar's statuesque grandeur but with the accompanying descriptions of people who should be far inferior to the general. He is frail while the charwoman is *robuste,* and his inglorious entrance contrasts with the imperturbable *valets solennels.* The hero is further reduced to an object as the servant screams: "Laissez donc! on ne touche ça qu'avec le balai." (290) Her final words are a sorry contrast with Volmar's "fières paroles": "Eh! va donc, vieux décombre! Ce n'est pas moi qui suis allé te chercher, bien sûr, vieille charogne!" (290)

France handles the story's many transformation scenes with great skill. The basic happy/sad opposition is frequently presented in terms of a literal rising and falling action. The most striking before-and-after portrait is of M. du Bocage:

> Quatrefeuilles et Saint-Sylvain trouvèrent M. du Bocage dormant dans un fauteuil, la bouche retroussée jusqu'aux pommettes, les narines dilatées, les joues rondes et rayonnantes comme deux soleils, la poitrine harmonieuse, le ventre rythmique et paisible, riant, transpirant la joie depuis la voûte étincelante du crâne jusqu'aux orteils en éventail dans de légers escarpins, au bout des jambes écartées. (264)

The description of the sleeping man is filled with images of upward or expansive movement: his turned-up mouth, the *voûte* of his gleaming, bald head; the beams radiating from his cheeks and his fanned-out toes. His whole being emanates joy, true to Rodrigue's theory. In contrast, when he is awakened "toute sa personne exprimait l'ennui, le regret et la déception," and this sadness is characterized by verbs of downward movement:

> Les coins de sa bouche *s'abaissaient;* ses joues *tombaient,* ses paupières *pendaient* comme du linge aux fenêtres des pauvres. (264; italics mine)

France does not overuse this technique. In some transformations it is eliminated entirely; in others, used only briefly, as in the description of the frustrated Prince de Lusance: "Et, quittant la fenêtre, il s'abîma dans un fauteuil." (297) France even parodies his own technique with the exaggerated description of M. de Granthosme, who is so literally depressed that his downward gaze is fixed on Quatrefeuilles' feet:

> ... ses gros yeux pâles lui tombaient au milieu des joues; son nez lui pendait sur la bouche. Il semblait abîmé de douleur et regardait avec affliction les pieds de Quatrefeuilles. (297)

The episode also varies the happy/unhappy paradigm by presenting the portrait of the unhappy man initially. The contrast in this case is not based on a transformation but rather on the surprising identification of the unhappy character as one who should, objectively, be happy: "Je ne suis pas bottier, répondit l'étranger plein d'une humble douceur, je suis le marquis de Granthosme." [18] The same technique is used for another wealthy character, "Jacques Feligne-Cobur, qui possédait des montagnes d'or, des mines de diamant, des mers de pétrole." (293) While seeking entry to his vast estate, Quatrefeuilles and Saint-Sylvain meet a poor "cantonnier" who "redressa péniblement sa maigre échine et tourna vers eux son visage creux, masqué de lunettes grillées. —Monsieur Jacques Felgine-Cobur, c'est moi, dit-il." (293-94) The "C'est moi" construction (rather than a declarative "Je suis...") maintains the suspense to the last possible moment.

France builds suspense by varying the timing of his transitions. The composer, Sigismund Dux, seems entirely happy; indeed, Quatrefeuilles has almost completed his request for the musician's shirt when the transformation occurs:

> —Maître, donnez-moi votre che...
> Il s'arrêta, voyant les traits de Sigismond Dux subitement décomposés. (322)

---

[18] *Ibid.*, 298. The duc de Volmar episode combines the techniques of transformation and belated identification.

In the case of Jeronimo, the reader is given a false alarm. The politician had been chatting happily when he was approached by a certain foreign minister: "Aussitôt Jeronimo se transforma." (274) But this transformation is not a change for the worse; on the contrary, Jeronimo becomes the epitome of the skillful and successful diplomat. It is only after Jeronimo's vulgar good humor is contrasted with aristocratic simplicity that the definitive transformation occurs:

> Tandis qu'ils parlaient ainsi, Jeronimo se promenait, le chapeau sur l'oreille, faisait le moulinet avec sa canne, répandait son humeur hilare en plaisanteries, en badinages, en rires, en exclamations, en mauvais jeux de mots, en calembours obscènes et scatalogiques, en fredons. Cependant, à quinze pas devant lui, le duc des Aulnes, arbitre des élégances et prince de la jeunesse, rencontrant une dame de sa connaissance, la salua très simplement d'un petit geste sec, mais non sans grâce. Le tribun l'observa d'un regard attentif, puis, devenu sombre et songeur, il abattit sa main pesante sur l'épaule de son échassier:
> —Jobelin, lui dit-il, je donnerais ma popularité et dix ans de ma vie pour porter le frac et parler aux femmes comme ce freluquet.
> Il avait perdu sa gaieté. Il allait maintenant, morne, la tête basse...[19]

The happy/unhappy status of another character, Jacques de Navicelle, is left pending and the problem is resolved only after Quatrefeuilles and Saint-Sylvain have abandoned their inquiry:

> Sans doute il était aimé; en était-il heureux ou malheureux? Quand on apporta les fruits, les deux inquisiteurs du roi renonçaient à le savoir. (311)

The repeated contrasts and oppositions of "La Chemise" cannot really be resolved. They result in a kind of frustrated equilibrium which is reinforced stylistically by a number of verbal

---

[19] France, XIX, 275-76. Jeronimo's expansive vulgarity is reflected in the sentence by the multiple verbs and prepositional objects, while the duke's elegance is indicated by the succinct description of his *petit geste sec*. Jeronimo's transition to sorrow is described in terms of weight and downward movement: il *abattit* sa main *pesante*; il allait... la tête *basse*.

balances. The equilibrium created by pairs of opposing characters is often emphasized by tightly-drawn comparisons and elegantly balanced syntax, as in the case of the two court physicians. A similar verbal balance can be seen in the description of two politicians who stand symbolically beneath the statue of Fortune:

> Ils sont *tous deux* infortunés, lui dit-il; *l'un* ne se console pas d'avoir perdu le pouvoir, *l'autre* tremble de le perdre. Et leur ambition est d'autant plus misérable qu'ils sont *l'un et l'autre* plus libres et plus puissants dans une condition privée que dans l'exercice du pouvoir.... (272; italics mine)

Positive action, too, is often stymied. Christophe's relations with his factory workers are characterized by a state of negative equilibrium:

> Il ne les soulageait point ni ne les opprimait davantage, afin qu'ils fussent toujours une menace et jamais un danger. (274)

And aside from its Rabelaisian anti-medical humor, Christophe's illness and its treatment remain in a state of balance. The doctors hold a "mésestime réciproque" of each other's qualifications and therefore switch opinions, "sachant qu'ils n'y risquaient rien et ne perdraient ni ne gagneraient au change, puisque c'étaient des opinions médicales." (251) Their prescriptions remain "également vains" and have no effect on the king: "Il n'en allait pas plus mal, mais il n'en allait pas mieux." (256) France describes Christophe's condition elsewhere with another verbal equilibrium: "sa faiblesse croissait chaque jour sans diminuer sa capacité de souffrir." (258) And madame de la Poule, too, remains suspended between two opposing forces: "Elle ressentait l'effroi de mourir et l'attrait du suicide." (312)

This lack of movement weighs upon the characters. Christophe V is sadly aware that nothing ever changes, to the point that change itself becomes monotony:

> En femmes il eût toujours aimé la nouveauté; mais une femme nouvelle n'était plus une nouveauté pour lui et la monotonie du changement lui pesait. De dépit, il retour-

nait à madame de la Poule et ce "déjà vu" qui lui était fastidieux chez celles qu'il voyait pour la première fois, il le supportait moins mal chez une vieille amie. [20]

This kind of circular development can be seen in other episodes as well. Things are not only contrasted with their opposites, they become their opposites. Hunting, for example, is an "antique nécessité devenue un divertissement, fatigue dont les grands se font un plaisir." (278) Virtue is defined as a vice and happiness is treated as if it were a crime:

> Le préfet de police, déférant à l'invitation du ministre, mit ses plus habiles agents au service des commissaires et bientôt, dans la capitale, les heureux furent recherchés avec autant de zèle et d'ardeur que, dans les autres pays, les malfaiteurs et les anarchistes.... (325)

France does provide some relief from these repeated patterns of contrast and arrested action. The episode of the "Salons de la ville" is presented in terms of progression rather than opposition; nevertheless, it is appropriately a progression *de mal en pire:*

> Ils y trouvèrent monsieur et madame Souppe *malheureux* de n'être pas reçus chez madame Esterlin, femme du maître des forges, député au parlement. Ils allèrent chez madame Esterlin, et l'y trouvèrent *désolée*, ainsi que M. Esterlin, de n'être pas reçus chez madame du Colombier, femme du pair du royaume, ancien ministre de la Justice. Ils allèrent chez madame du Colombier et y trouvèrent le pair et la pairesse *enragés* de n'être pas dans l'intimité de la reine. (301; italics mine)

This progression from bad to worse is reinforced by an accelerated repetition: "Les visiteurs qu'ils rencontrèrent dans ces diverses maisons n'étaient pas moins malheureux, désolés, enragés." (302) This is followed by another progressive element: "Les obscurs voulaient paraître, les illustres paraître davantage." (302) But this detail is particularly effective because it occurs within the frame-

---

[20] France, XIX, 248. Christophe's attitude is seconded by M. Sandrique, who realizes "combien l'esprit de conservation, de tradition, d'imitation et d'obéissance est fort dans les peuples et comme d'un train égal et lent va la vie sociale." (pp. 303-04)

work of a contrast (obscurs/illustres) and thus frustrates the reader's expectation of an opposition.

France frequently provides a link between these static characters and episodes by using the image of the line of vision as a device to simulate action or transition from one scene to another. The view from a window is a recurring technique. An elementary example is Quatrefeuilles' and Saint-Sylvain's observation of the courtiers:

> Ces deux gentilshommes pensèrent qu'ils pourraient se procurer le médicament du docteur Rodrigue sans quitter le palais, et se mirent à l'œil-de-bœuf d'où l'on voyait passer les courtisans. Ceux qu'ils aperçurent avaient la mine longue, le visage hâve; ils portaient leur mal écrit sur la figure; (264)

The bull's-eye window is quite fitting, since this is a limited and sharply focused view. In more elaborate examples, France starts with a general description; his view begins in the foreground and gradually focuses on a distant point. This kind of visual action provides the transition from the library scene to the duc de Volmar episode:

> Chaudesaigues hocha la tête, alla à la fenêtre et tambourina sur les vitres. Il pleuvait; la place d'armes était déserte. Au fond se dressait un palais magnifique dont l'attique était surmonté de trophées d'armes et qui portait à son fronton une Bellone casquée d'un hydre, cuirassée d'écailles et brandissant un glaive romain.
> —Allez dans ce palais, dit-il enfin. (284)

The same technique is used to trigger the transformation of the prince de Lusance:

> —Quelle belle vue! s'écrièrent Quatrefeuilles et Saint-Sylvain.
> Des terrasses, chargées de statues, d'orangers et de fleurs, conduisaient par de lents et faciles escaliers à la pelouse bordée de charmille et aux bassins où l'eau jaillissait en gerbes blanches des conques des tritons et des urnes des nymphes. A droite et à gauche une mer de verdure étendait ses houles apaisées jusqu'à la rivière loin-

> taine dont on suivait le fil argenté entre les peupliers, sous les collines enveloppées de brumes roses.
>
> Naguère souriant, le prince attachait un regard soucieux sur un point de cette vaste et belle étendue. (296)

The structure of France's *conte philosophique* is very similar to Voltaire's *Le Monde comme il va*. In the Voltairian tale, society's evils are contrasted with its advantages and a final balance is represented by a statue made of precious jewels and base metals. The unifying theme is not a quest but rather the threat of annihilation, to be visited by an avenging angel. Nevertheless, the mechanism of the two stories is identical. The favorable or unfavorable recommendation of Babouc, Voltaire's protagonist, corresponds to the alternately hopeful and disillusioned appraisals of Quatrefeuilles and Saint-Sylvain. These repeated commentaries serve as transitions between otherwise unrelated episodes. Voltaire's *Zadig* has also been compared to "La Chemise." Each of Zadig's successes is balanced by a subsequent misfortune, and each adventure is qualified by an observation on the possibility or impossibility of being happy. The uniformity and repetition of such a dialectical structure tends to slow the tempo of Voltaire's story.[21] France, in contrast, capitalizes on this structure. Unlike Voltaire, his wit is characterized by elaboration and digression rather than brevity.

France's tendency for digression can be seen in the following brief comparison. The inevitable contrast is postponed by a diverting commentary:

> J'ai vu le prince des Estelles malheureux parce que sa femme le trompe, non qu'il l'aime, mais il a de l'amour-propre, et le duc de Mauvert malheureux de ce que sa femme ne le trompe pas et le frustre ainsi des moyens de relever sa maison ruinée. Celui-ci est excédé par ses enfants; celui-là se désespère de n'en pas avoir... (277)

The psychological and financial motives of the two aristocrats lend an offbeat interest to an otherwise banal situation.

---

[21] See, e.g. Sareil, "De *Zadig* à *Candide*," *Romanic Review*, LII, No. 4 (December, 1961), pp. 271-278.

The description of Froidefond, with its disjunctive accumulation of pejorative details intruding between the subject and the verb, is a good example of how basic this technique is to France's style:

> Mais Quatrefeuilles, qui se défiait du raisonnement et n'en croyait, en toutes choses, que l'expérience, s'approcha de la table où Froidefond, dans un amas de bouquins recouverts de veau, de basane, de maroquin, de vélin, de parchemin, de peau de truie, d'ais de bois, sentant la poussière, le moisi, le rat et la souris, cataloguait. (281)

The relative length of France's version of "La Chemise" and earlier versions of the story (or indeed, of most *contes philosophiques*) is indicative of this difference in style. "La Chemise" is not built on the rapid accumulation of comic elements, like the more successful Voltairian stories. It rests on the elaboration of a single paradox, and France deliberately postpones the inevitable punch line. Indeed, the story's interest lies in this diversion of the reader's attention. France uses various forms of diversionary tactics. Characters tell stories within the story — Jeronimo's ribald tales, Quatrefeuilles' and Saint-Sylvain's social gossip. Episodes are interrupted for the development of a sub-plot, as in the introduction of the young farmer into the sequence dealing with the curé Miton.

At times, France deliberately weighs down the narrative with repetitive commentaries. Saint-Sylvain is a pedant, and his long string of quotations is typical of his mentality:

> Si La Galissonnière consultait un bon père jésuite, il serait bientôt rassuré, et Larive-du-Mont devrait savoir qu'on peut être athée avec sérénité comme Lucrèce, avec délices comme André Chénier. Qu'il se répète les vers d'Homère: "Patrocle est mort qui valait mieux que toi," et consente de meilleure grâce à rejoindre un jour ou l'autre ses maîtres les philosophes de l'antiquité, les humanistes de la Renaissance, les savants modernes et tant d'autres qui valaient mieux que lui "Et meurent Pâris et Hélène," dit François Villon. "Nous sommes tous mortels," comme dit Cicéron. "Nous mourons tous," dit cette femme dont l'Ecriture a loué la prudence au second livre des Rois. (307-08)

In contrast, France also sprinkles his text with totally irrelevant and bizarre details, like Madame de la Poule's mysterious convulsions or M. de Quatrefeuilles' peripatetic stomach! Amusing names are another source of diversion. They range from the mildly obscene (the galant professor Quillebœuf) to the ridiculous (the royal mistress, madame de la Poule) to the self-evident (the wealthy marquis de Granthosme, the bourgeois madame Souppe, and the happiness-seeking Quatrefeuilles).

France also diverts the reader with pastiches of various literary styles or movements. Some are obvious, like Jacques de Navicelle's *conte oriental*. Others are more subtle. The prince de Lausance ("un délicat") resembles Huysmans' Des Esseintes in his attempts at synesthesia:

> Je vais vous avouer ma manie, dit le prince de Lusance. Parfois, quand je suis seul, je joue devant des tableaux et j'ai l'illusion de traduire par des sons l'harmonie des couleurs et des lignes. Devant ce portrait, j'essaye de rendre la ferme caresse du dessin et, découragé, je laisse mon violon. [22]

The description of brutal peasant life, dominated by the "natural needs" for food and love, is an echo of Zola's *La Terre:*

> La faim et l'amour, ces deux fléaux de la nature, y frappaient les malheureux humains à coups plus forts et plus pressés. Ils virent des maîtres avares, des maris jaloux, des femmes menteuses, des servantes empoisonneuses, des valet assassins, des pères incestueux, des enfants qui renversaient la huche sur la tête de l'aïeul, sommeillant à l'angle du foyer. Ces paysans ne trouvaient de plaisir que dans l'ivresse; leur joie même était brutale, leurs jeux cruels. Leurs fêtes se terminaient en rixes sanglantes.
>
> A mesure qu'ils les observaient davantage, Quatrefeuilles et Saint-Sylvain reconnaissaient que les mœurs de ces hommes ne pouvaient être ni meilleures ni plus pures, que la terre avare les rendait avares, qu'une dure vie les endurcissait aux maux d'autrui comme aux leurs, que s'ils était jaloux, cupides, faux, menteurs, sans cesse occupés à se tromper les uns les autres, c'était l'effet naturel de leur indigence et de leur misère. (331-32)

---

[22] France, XIX, 296. The violin and Ingres portrait are also a pun on the common expression "violon d'Ingres."

Finally, the young suicide (his hair blowing in the soft breeze under a starry sky) is a perfect romantic hero, suffering from "un grand malaise" and "le mal de vivre." (316)

In spite of these digressive elements, however, "La Chemise" in no way lacks unity or cohesion. One unifying device — a Voltairian technique — is the use of leitmotiv or repetition. For example, suspense is created by the repeated references to Dr. Rodrigue. At first, Saint-Sylvain repeatedly urges Christophe to see Rodrigue and the king refuses; then with a typical reversal of the action, it is Christophe himself who demands Rodrigue and fears that he will not come:

> —Sire, dit M. de Saint-Sylvain, premier secrétaire des commandements, consultez le docteur Rodrigue. (252)

> —Oui, Sire, dit M. de Quatrefeuilles, faites appeler le docteur Rodrigue. Il n'y a que cela à faire. (252)

> —Sire, lui dit M. de Saint-Sylvain, faites venir le docteur Rodrigue. Il vous guérira sûrement. (256)

> M. de Saint-Sylvain trouva l'occasion bonne pour recommander une fois encore le docteur Rodrigue, mais le roi déclara qu'il n'avait pas besoin d'un médecin de plus... (251)

> —Monsieur de Saint-Sylvain, dit-il un matin, après une mauvaise nuit, vous m'avez plusieurs fois parlé du docteur Rodrigue. Faites-le venir. (258)

Quatrefeuilles' gallstone is a parody of the king's illness but it is also continued as a humorous leitmotiv. The paradoy is developed even further by Saint-Sylvain's "stone" — his wife. The first topic automatically summons up the other, and this automatic response is itself a parody of social conversations:

> ...et bien que je porte le poids d'une vessie plus chargée de pierres qu'un tombereau au sortir de la carrière, il y a des jours où je suis amoureux comme à vingt ans.
> —Moi, répondit Saint-Sylvain, je suis misogyne. Je ne pardonne pas aux femmes d'être du même sexe que madame de Saint-Sylvain. (310)

> De guerre lasse, ils parlèrent pour ne rien dire, et parlèrent d'eux-mêmes: Saint-Sylvain de sa femme et Quatrefeuilles de sa pierre fondamentale... (311)

France also makes isolated references to earlier, humorous passages. These extended jokes, like the more developed refrains, help hold the story together. For example, doctor Macheillier's long-winded medical analogy is called to mind but a tedious repetition is avoided (since Christophe shares the reader's impatience with Machellier and interrupts him):

> —La neurasthénie, dit Machellier, véritable Protée pathologique...
> Mais le roi les congédia tous deux. (252)

And madame de la Poule's previous disguises are evoked by a passing comment:

> Christophe V passa l'été d'une façon supportable. Il fit une croisière à bord d'un yacht de deux cents tonneaux, avec madame de la Poule habillée en mousse. (257)

Unity also results from the expansion of Christophe's "symptoms." His illness is clearly symptomatic of modern society's ills at large. His spiritual malaise is characterized by the paradoxical (but normal, in France's context of opposition) effects of leisure and exertion:

> Toute occupation a pour moi le vide de l'oisiveté et le repos me lasse comme un pénible travail. (248)

The same effects are experienced by women in general, according to Saint-Sylvain, who "ne font rien, et se tuent de fatigue." (269) Aristocrats, too, suffer from these symptoms:

> Nos gentilshommes crèvent à la fois d'ennui et de tracas sur leurs terres; toujours en procès avec leurs voisins, dévorés par les hommes de loi, ils traînent dans les soucis leur pesante oisiveté. (277)

Christophe's physical symptoms are also repeated and reflected in the condition of his subjects. The king's ailments are quite explicit and realistic at first, but they become more and more figurative as his illness progresses:

> Il se plaignait de ce qu'une fourmilière s'était établie dans son cerveau et que cette colonie industrieuse et guerrière y creusait des galeries, des chambres, des magasins, y transportait des vivres, des matériaux, y déposait des œufs par milliards, y nourrissait les jeunes, y soutenait des sièges, donnait, repoussait des assauts, s'y livrait des combats acharnés. (256)

> Il me semble, leur dit un jour Christophe V étendu sur sa chaise longue, il me semble qu'une nichée de rats me grignotent les entrailles, pendant qu'un nain horrible, un kobold en capuchon, tunique et chausses rouges, descendu dans mon estomac, l'entame à coups de pic et le creuse profondément. (257)

Even at their most fantastic, however, Christophe's pains are described as a gnawing sensation, and this feeling is shared by his society — in his generals, whose jealousies "leur ravagent le foie," in Jeronimo, who reveals "la plaie qui le ronge," and in the entire bourgeoisie, beset by troubles which "les rongeaient."

"La Chemise" is one of France's strongest stories because its theme and structure are nearly parallel. Its pessimism is as much a function of structure as a philosophical *parti pris;* that is, the negative paradox is the basic mechanism of the narrative. France's conclusion should be viewed as a *reductio ad absurdum* and not a serious advocacy of the simple-minded felicity represented by his happy man. Perfect happiness, like the supernatural, is an ideal; it can only be corrupted by the contingencies of everyday life. But such as it is, full of contradictions and unpredictable, life is triumphant in "La Chemise": "la vie de cette terre, la vie telle qu'elle est, la chienne de vie." (306)

NOTE

The legend of the shirt of the happy man has been traced back to Greek tales and even linked with Buddhistic parables.[23] Variants

---

[23] See Reinhold Köhler, *Aufsätze über Märchen und Volkslieder*, Berlin, 1894.

of the story exist in the folklore of many European, Scandanavian and Asian countries. Casti's eighteenth-century version (originally published in Italian in Paris in 1793) seems inspired from the Tunesian rather than the Italian variant (the latter involves the shirt made by a happy woman and emphasizes the theme of consolation from grieving for a loved one by the inevitability of sorrow and death).

Casti's version, on the contrary, abandons the darker philosophical overtones. His witty and often risqué tale rejects the corruption of civilization and idealizes pastoral virtues. Casti was soon imitated in both English and French.[24] Daru's "Le Roi malade" appeared in 1803, only a few years after Casti's original edition of the *Novelle galanti*. Daru does not mention the Italian author, but Sir Walter Scott, in his "The Search after Happiness" (1817) acknowledges Casti. Both Scott and Daru made their versions of the story more "contemporary" — Scott, in political satire and Daru by substituting a happy worker for the happy shephard of Casti's tale.

Casti's *Novelle* and his *Animali parlanti* were extremely popular in France. It is very likely that Anatole France (who knew Italian and had traveled in Italy) would have read the works of the notorious abbé, an admirer and imitator of Voltaire whose gallant adventures and wordly tastes ressemble France's own Jérôme Coignard. Moreover, there are textual similarities which indicate that France had read Casti's tale. First, the amusing "mode d'emploi" of the curative shirt. Rodrigue specifies, "Faites-la légèrement chauffer ... avant de vous en servir." (262) Casti also stipulates warmth: "E calda calda indosso se gli metta."[25] Daru and Scott do not include this detail. Casti's tale also suggests the differences in theory and practice held by the two searchers. His Satrap and courtier (like Quatrefeuilles and Saint-Sylvain) quarrel over the theoretical capacity of the poor to be happy (cantos XLII,

---

[24] This theme, taken from Ser Giovanni's *Pecorone* (giornata ii, nov. 1) was translated into French and English and enjoyed considerable popularity in the eighteenth century. Nineteenth-century French versions of the story include L'Orgeril's "Le Charme," published in 1885, and d'Avenel's rendition of a Tunesian variant of the tale (1883) [cited by Köhler] — but these probably have no direct link with Casti.

[25] Giovanni Battista Casti, *Novelle* (Paris, 1804), I, 52.

XLIII). They also reject philosophical speculation in favor of direct observation: "Disinganniam le astratte idee: si vada."[26]

Despite these similarities, however, Casti's tale in no way acts as a sounding board for France's ideas as Perrault's tales or the song of St. Nicolas do in the preceding stories.

---

[26] *Ibid.*, 41.

# CONCLUSION

Irony is one of the most striking characteristics of Anatole France's artistic vision. It is a persistently double perception, shifting between what is said and what is intended. France's irony in *Les Sept Femmes de la Barbe-Bleue* is directed against his protagonists, his narrator and the reader: all are involved in a system of frustrated expectations. Paradox and parody are used in these stories as humorous expressions of this ironic mentality.

France's ironic vision takes the form of shifting patterns of reality. He plays on the definition of the real and the imaginary, contrasting the physical world with the supernatural and intellectual processes with material contingencies. The humor of the stories lies in the tension created between these opposing poles as well as the reversal of habitual perceptions. It is a subtle trick, like the reversing fields of an optical illusion.

The tension of France's fundamentally ironic viewpoint is reflected in the paradoxical relationships on which the stories are based. "Les Sept Femmes de la Barbe-Bleue," "Le Grand Saint Nicolas," and "L'Histoire de la duchesse de Cicogne et de M. de Boulingrin" all hinge on the relationship of the real and the supernatural (the *merveilleux* of the title): if the supernatural is real then it is non-existent; it exists only so long as it is not real. The final story, "La Chemise," is premised on a similar paradox. Perfect happiness is impossible: therefore the sought-after remedy cannot exist. The shirt of a happy man is the cure for melancholia only if such a shirt cannot be found. (And it is worth noting that in the alternate ending to Casti's version of the tale, the unhappy king is presented with the magic shirt and throws it into the sea.)

## CONCLUSION

A paradox is an explicit yet inexplicable conflict. Two contrasting or even mutually contradictory propositions are presented, to which we are led by apparently valid arguments. The solving of a genuine paradox may require a re-examination of our fundamental logical processes in order to explain the contradiction. Most paradoxes, however, are semantic rather than logical; that is, due "not to any fault in logic, but to the vagueness or ambiguity of some non-logical aspect"[1] such as truth, definability, or language. These weak links of rational thought are deliberately shown at their worst in France's apparent paradoxes. These paradoxes can also be called ironic, because they express France's inherently double perception as well as his conscious imposition of rational terminology on irrational phenomena.

There is another kind of ironic paradox in these stories, however: false paradoxes which involve France's parodic transformations of traditional texts; and the irony in these paradoxes is represented on a structural level as well. Parodies are usually implicit contrasts. They involve a distortion rather than complete destruction of a pattern. In parody there is no hesitation between the model and the imitation; the parody is a burlesque version of the original model. Parody can be compared to the reflection in a trick mirror: it must be a recognizable likeness of the original and yet it must deviate from the model at strategic moments. If it is too faithful a representation there is imitation but no humor; if the deviation is too great there is grotesqueness but no contrast.

France's parodies are used as one of the conflicting elements in a humorous paradox. He confronts the "authoritative" models for his stories and attempts to discredit them with his new (and parodic) interpretations. Both the parody and the original story claim validity. This confrontation is ironic, however; there is a deliberate flaw in the presentation of the parody and the conundrum thus proves to be an illusion. These are false paradoxes because one of the elements in the contrast is invalid.

These paradoxical parodies are doubly ironic because they are used as a smoke screen for France's criticism of historical research

---

[1] Paul Edwards, Ed., *The Encyclopedia of Philosophy*, (New York: Macmillan & The Free Press, 1967), V, 45.

and rational objectivity. France is trying to amuse his readers with these paradoxes rather than convince them of their validity. He proposes a series of clever contradictions: an innocent Bluebeard, a guilty Saint Nicolas, a credulous skeptic; and he presents plausible arguments to support his thesis. At the same time, however, he clearly undermines these arguments. And this ironic treatment of rational and scientific methods — which works as a process of demystification for the reader — is of primary interest. While France's protagonists remain embroiled in their paradoxical circumstances, the reader grasps the irony of the situation and appreciates the play between reality and appearance.

France is not trying to "prove" Bluebeard's innocence any more than he is seriously disturbed by Mouque's lack of a shirt. He uses parody and paradox to whet the reader's interest and takes advantage of the immediate process of demystification (the unraveling of the false paradox) to disabuse the reader of some other misconceptions as well, namely the premises of scientific methodology. The paradox has been called an "intellectual gadfly"[2] and France's use of them fits this definition. Their sting is good-natured, though, and the ultimate effect (after the pretense of a *mise en cause*) is a reaffirmation of the Cartesian principles of reason and logic.

---

[2] Edwards, *op. cit.*, p. 51.

# APPENDIX

The complex ironic structure of *Les Sept Femmes de la Barbe-Bleue* becomes more evident if these stories are compared with France's non-parodic fairy tales. His only serious attempt at the genre is a story entitled "Abeille." The story is contemporary with the "Dialogue sur les contes de fées" and although it was a distinct failure with the public, it is a good illustration of the kind of tale which France admired in that theoretical discussion. To the extent that all fairy tales are allegorical, "Abeille" contains a message: the preference for art rather than science (which is expressed in the "Dialogue...") as well as various moral platitudes. But "Abeille" is presented at face value: neither character nor plot is used primarily as a foil to deflect France's irony.

The stories in *Les Sept Femmes...* are not themselves fairy tales or saint's legends; they take existing genres as a *point de départ*. The analysis of France's stories thus focused on his use of those genres rather than their characteristics. In the case of "Abeille," a brief discussion of the fairy tale would be useful. "Abeille" can be called a fairy tale because — within certain limits — it respects the conceits of style which are characteristic of that genre. As Todorov points out, it is not simply the subject matter (supernatural beings) which makes a story a fairy tale, but rather a "certaine écriture."[1]

Fairy tales can be distinguished from realistic, strange or fantastic literature by their treatment of the supernatural.[2] Marvel-

---

[1] Tzvetan Todorov, *Introduction à la littérature fantastique* (Paris: Editions du Seuil, 1970), p. 59.

[2] See Todorov, *op. cit*, p. 59: "Dans le cas du merveilleux, les éléments surnaturels ne provoquent aucune réaction particulière ni chez les person-

ous characters and events are completely normal in the context of the fairy tale; they are not noteworthy simply by virtue of being supernatural but only insofar as they benefit or thwart the hero. In fact, the moral theme of the story (either in the form of a concluding moral or interspersed in the narration) is often just as important to the fairy tale as the supernatural; and it is possible to have very naturalistic fairy tales, like George Sand's *Contes d'une grand'mère,* in which the supernatural is often completely rationalized. The moral and supernatural content of fairy tales is thus variable, ranging from the fantasy of the *Mille et une nuits* to the thinly disguised moralizing of Madame Leprince de Beaumont or Madame d'Aulnoy.

The fairy tale is often based on folk tale, but it is a literary form whose definitive version can be credited to a single author. In a "pure" fairy tale, that is, one that is closest to the folk tale model, the author calls no attention to the narration. The story is brief; details are limited and generally symbolic.[3] Length and profusion of detail are the two areas in which France's style diverges considerably from traditional fairy tales. Brevity alone, however, does not guarantee authenticity. Perrault's classic tales, although brief, are a highly sophisticated form of the fairy tale because both the moral and supernatural aspects of the stories are treated ironically. His stories are meant to be humorous, and heroes and villains alike are the subject of facetious remarks. In this respect, France's parodies in *Les Sept Femmes*... are much closer in spirit to Perrault than "Abeille."

The distinction between "Abeille" and *Les Sept Femmes*... is primarily one of expression rather than structure. It would be possible, for example, to isolate certain patterns of narrative structure in the folk tale or fairy tale,[4] but obviously an "authentic" story

---

nages, ni chez le lecteur implicite. Ce n'est pas une attitude envers les événements rapportés qui caractérise le merveilleux, mais la nature même de ces événements."

[3] See Luthi, *op. cit.*, for a discussion of the style of the fairy tale.

[4] Using, e.g. Bremond's refinement of Propp's functional theory. Nevertheless, as Bremond points out, these structural sequences would be applicable to many kinds of narratives (literary and non-literary) and tend to create a general model of the narrative rather than a specific model of the folk tale such as Propp had envisaged.

and a parody of that story would have identical structures. Thus the same arrangement of functional sequences would be found in the traditional Bluebeard story, in Perrault's "La Barbe-bleue" and even in France's version of the tale, but the amount of irony in each story clearly distinguishes one from the other on the level of narrative technique. There is no consistently ironic treatment of the elements of the action in "Abeille": no complicity of the narrator and reader at the expense of the characters. This is not to say that the story is devoid of ironic elements; but for the most part the irony is directed against one character by another.

The plot and characters of "Abeille" — a princess kidnapped by benevolent dwarfs — have only the slightest similarity to traditional themes in French folklore.[5] Dwarfs, in particular, are conspicuously absent from the French folk tale,[6] as are most grotesque or monstrous creatures.[7] The Snow White story is the best-known tale of the rescue/abduction of a human maiden by dwarfs; but in the French version of the tale, "Blanche-Neige," the woods-dwellers are twelve human brothers rather than dwarfs. Moreover, the plot of "Abeille" has no similarity with Snow White.

Dwarfs abound in Germanic and Northern European folk tales, and France's dwarfs reflect many of the general traits which are found in this traditional literature: dwarfs are little men with large heads and long beards; they are helpful, intelligent, sensible and wise; they are industrious workmen (particularly as metal-smiths); they possess vast treasures, and they have been known to kidnap mortals.[8]

Although there is no specific folk tale which parallels "Abeille," France has tried to create the impression of an oral narrative in his text. Twenty-five sentences in the narrative (excluding dialogue) begin with "Et" and another half-dozen begin with "Alors."

---

[5] See Paul Delarue, *op. cit.* Broad analogies could be drawn with his type 301 (Les Princesses délivrées du monde souterrain), 307 (La Princesse délivrée), and 316 (L'Enfant promis à la sirène).

[6] Mme. d'Aulnoy's Nain Jaune is a notable exception. Le Petit Poucet is not a dwarf (an underground spirit) but a thumbling or pygmy.

[7] See e.g. Delarue, "Les Caractères propres du conte populaire français," *La Pensée* (Mars-avril, 1957), pp. 40-62.

[8] In Stith Thompson, ed., *Motif Index of Folk Literature*, III (Bloomington, Indiana: Indiana University Press, 1956), section F451, pp. 103ff.

Within the dialogue, the repetition of the phrase "Petit roi Loc" and ("vous tous, petits hommes") becomes a constant echo. France also adopts the story-teller's techniques of foreshadowing and summary, and the "listener" is reminded of past details when an abandoned storyline is taken up again.

Several passages are obviously intended to be read aloud (or to give that impression). The most subdued of these passages is the dwafs' shouldering of Abeille's litter:

> L'ayant recouvert de mousse et de feuillée, ils y firent asseoir Abeille; puis ils saisirent à la fois les deux montants, ohé! se les mirent sur l'épaule, hop! et prirent leur course vers la montagne, hip! [9]

The interjections are multiplied in the lively description of the dwarfs' contagious laughter: the repetitive "ha! ha!'s" do create a visual echo effect.

> Tout le long de son chemin, il se tint le ventre pour rire à son aise: son chef en branlait; sa barbe allait et venait sur son estomac. —Ha! ha! ha! ha! ha! ha! ha! —Les petits hommes qui le rencontraient se mettaient à rire comme lui, par sympathie. En les voyant rire, les autres riaient aussi; ce rire gagna de proche en proche, en sorte que tout l'intérieur de la terre fut secoué par un hoquet extrêmement jovial. Ha! ha! ha! ha! ha! ha! ha! ha! ha! ha! ha! ha! ha! ha! ha! ha! (314)

France's tone is even more mimetic in the description of the old woman, Maurille, feeding her hens:

> Elle criait: "Psit! psit! psit! petits! petits! petits! psit! psit! psit!" et elle jetait du grain à ses poussins.
> —Psit! psit! psit! petits! petits! petits! C'est vous, monseigneur? Psit! psit! psit! Est-ce possible que vous soyez devenu si beau? Psit! psit! chu! chu! chu! (336)

However, the attempt to recreate aural effects is less successful in the saccherine bird-song which celebrates Georges' return:

---

[9] France, "Abeille," in *Balthasar, Œuvres* (Paris: Calmann-Lévy, 1925), IV, 277. Hereafter cited as *Abeille*. All further references to this text will be given parenthetically whenever possible.

> Cui cui, cui
> Oui, oui, oui,
> Georges de Blanchelande,
> Cui, cui, cui,
> Dont vous avez nourri l'enfance,
> Cui, cui, cui,
> Est ici, ici, ici!
> Oui, oui, oui. (332)
>
> Cependant, les oiseaux chantaient:
> Cuicui, cui, i, cui, cui, cui,
> Oui, oui, oui, oui, oui, oui.
> Il est ici, ici, ici, ici, ici, ici! (333)

France's text includes many realistic details which are typical of the common sense and resourcefulness of fairy-tale heroes. For example, Abeille's candor with the dwarfs is quite down-to-earth: "Petits hommes, il est dommage que vous soyez si laids; mais je vous aimerai tout de même si vous me donnez à manger, car j'ai faim." (275)

On the other hand, realistic details can contribute to an atmosphere of the fantastic. Real objects can become mysterious depending on how they are described. Exaggerated dimensions turn crustaceans into monsters:

> Des crabes *énormes,* des langoustes et des homards *géants,* des araignées de mer craquaient sous les pieds du Nain, puis s'en allaient en abandonnant quelqu'une de leurs pattes et réveillaient dans leur fuite des limules hideux, des poulpes *séculaires* qui soudain agitèrent leurs *cent* bras et crachaient de leur bec d'oiseau un poison fétide. (324; italics mine)

Similarly, the flora and fauna of the lake shore are particularly exotic because of discordant adjectives: flowers are described in terms of animal properties and birds in terms of inanimate phenomena:

> ... les nénufars étalaient leurs grandes feuilles en *cœur* et leurs fleurs à la *chair* blanche. Sur ces îles fleuries, les demoiselles, aux corsages d'*émeraude* ou de *saphir* et aux ailes de *flamme,* traçaient d'un vol strident des courbes brusquement brisées (264; italics mine)

In other cases, the mere profusion of real objects results in an impression of the marvelous. King Loc's treasure is fantastic because it is so extensively described; all of the objects are real but many are archaic and hence even more exotic. This enumeration is very different in effect from the facetious catalogs in "Le Grand Saint Nicolas":

> Pendus aux colonnes, d'immenses boucliers d'or recevaient les rayons du soleil et les renvoyaient en gerbes étincelantes; des épées, des lances s'entrecroisaient, ayant une flamme à leur pointe. Des tables qui régnaient autour des murailles étaient chargées de hanaps, de buires, d'aiguières, de calices, de ciboires, de patènes, de gobelets et de vidrecomes d'or, de cornes à boire en ivoire avec des anneaux d'argent, de bouteilles énormes en cristal de roche, de plats d'or et d'argent ciselé, de coffrets, de reliquaires en forme d'église, de cassolettes, de miroirs, de candélabres et de torchères aussi admirables par le travail que par la matière, et de brûle-parfums représentant des monstres. Et l'on distinguait sur une des tables un jeu d'échecs en pierre de lune.[10]

The singling out of a unique *objet d'art* heightens the effect of the enumeration. This effect is then intensified by the listing of still more treasures. Even humble kitchen utensils are enhanced by this technique, and the wealth of the "Ile des Perles et des Montagnes d'Or" extends to the château kitchen in an awesome profusion of pots and pans:

> Casseroles, poêles, poêlons, chaudrons, coquemars, fours de campagne, grils, sauteuses, lèche-frites, cuisinières, poissonières, bassins, moules à pâtisserie, cruches de cuivre, hanaps d'or et d'argent et de madre madré, sans compter le tournebroche de fer artistement forgé et la marmite ample et noire suspendue à la crémaillère. (251)

At the same time that realism approaches the marvelous, the supernatural is treated in a completely normal fashion (in true fairy tale style). France establishes the reality of the supernatural in the very first sentence, where the identity of the count of

---

[10] *Abeille*, 290-91. See *supra*, 70-71.

Blanchelande's slayer is simply the last in a series of realistic details:

> Ayant mis sur ses cheveux d'or un chaperon noir brodé de perles et noué à sa taille les cordelières des veuves, la comtesse de Blanchelande entre dans l'oratoire où elle avait coutume de prier chaque jour pour l'âme de son mari, tué en combat singulier par un géant d'Irlande. (233)

The description of the duchy of Les Clarides provides additional details of a supernatural nature:

> Son duché comprenait une grande surface de terres avec des landes dont les bruyères couvraient l'étendue désolée, des lacs où les pêcheurs prenaient des poissons dont quelques-uns étaient magiques, et des montagnes qui s'élevaient dans des solitudes horribles au-dessus des régions habitées par les Nains. (238)

Giants, magic fish, and dwarfs are perfectly acceptable: the dual universe of the fairy tale is natural and supernatural. Signs, predictions and spirits are also normal occurances. The countess recognizes the portent of her impending death in "une rose blanche sur le coussin de son prie-Dieu." (233) Moreover, her friend, the duchess, also accepts the validity of the omen: "La duchesse n'ignorait pas ce que la rose blanche annonce aux dames de Blanchelande." (235) She, in turn, predicts the future union of their children, and is not at all surprised when a supernatural creature reiterates her prophecy:

> —Il la défendra, dit la mère de Georges.
> —Et elle l'aimera, répondit la mère d'Abeille.
> —Elle l'aimera, répéta une petite voix claire que la duchesse reconnut pour celle d'un Esprit logé depuis longtemps sous une pierre du foyer. (235)

The existence and power of the dwarfs, established in the opening pages, is reinforced by the story of the old woman (whose former status is itself an element of the supernatural):

> J'ai été reine de l'Ile des Perles et des Montagnes d'Or; j'avais chaque jour quatorze sortes de poissons à ma table, et un négrillon me portait ma queue.

> —Et par quel malheur avez-vous perdu vos îles et vos montagnes, bonne femme? demanda la duchesse.
> —J'ai mécontenté les Nains, qui m'ont transportée loin de mes états. (248)

The old woman's tale also serves as a dramatic preparation for the children's adventures.

The reality of the supernatural is never seriously challenged in the story. France develops suspense by temporarily suggesting that the supernatural beings are simply figments of the children's imagination:

> Ce sont des voleurs ou plutôt des ogres, pensaient-ils. En réalité, c'étaient des gardes que la duchesse des Clarides avait envoyés à la recherche des deux petits aventureux. (263)

> —Ce sont des pieds de diablotins, dit Abeille.
> —Ou de biches, dit Georges. La chose n'a point été éclairée. (263-64)

> Abeille s'avança sur le sable entre deux bouquets de saules, et devant elle le petit Génie du lieu sauta dans l'eau en laissant à la surface des cercles qui s'agrandirent et s'effacèrent. Ce Génie était une petite grenouille verte au ventre blanc. (265)

But this doubt only serves to reinforce the reality of the dwarfs and water nymphs. The first appearance of the dwarfs seems to be another example of an overactive imagination; but Abeille's vision is real:

> Abeille, étendue, les mains jointes, sur son lit de mousse, vit les étoiles s'allumer en tremblant dans le ciel pâle; puis ses yeux se fermèrent à demi; pourtant il lui sembla voir en l'air un petit Nain monté sur un corbeau. Ce n'était point une illusion. (266)

Unlike M. de Boulingrin, Abeille is forced to accept the fact that her encounter with the supernatural is completely real:

> Quand elle se vit sur un lit de mousse, entourée de Nains, elle crut que ce qu'elle voyait était un rêve de la nuit et elle frotta ses yeux pour les dessiller, et afin qu'il y entrât,

> au lieu de la vision fantastique, la pure lumière du matin visitant sa chambre bleue, où elle croyait être. Car son esprit, engourdi par le sommeil, ne lui rappelait pas l'aventure du lac. Mais elle avait beau se frotter les yeux, les Nains n'en sortaient pas; il lui fallu bien croire qu'ils étaient véritables. (274)

Georges' experience, too, passes from phenomena which appear natural (like Abeille's dreaming) to the supernatural. At first he sees the reflection of the moonlight on the lake; then doubt is aroused:

> Georges vit bien que ces lueurs qui éclairaient les eaux n'étaient pas toutes le reflet brisé de la lune, car il remarqua des flammes bleues qui s'avançaient en tournoyant avec des ondulations et des balancements comme si elles dansaient des rondes. (266)

Finally, the suggested supernatural aspect of the lights ("comme si elles dansaient des rondes") is confirmed:

> Il reconnut bientôt que ces flammes tremblaient sur des fronts blancs, sur des fronts de femmes. En peu de temps, de belles têtes couronnées d'algues et de pétoncles, des épaules sur lesquelles se répandaient des chevelures vertes, des poitrines brillantes de perles, et d'où glissaient des voiles, s'élevèrent au-dessus des vagues. L'enfant reconnut les Ondines et voulut fuir. (267)

The identification of the supernatural is developed gradually: Georges first distinguishes *des fronts,* then *des fronts de femmes* (women, even though their attire may be bizarre, are mortal); and at last he calls the creatures by name, *les Ondines.*

Magic thus becomes "normal" in the context of the story. Magic spells are noteworthy only in terms of their function. They can be either helpful or harmful to the hero. Abeille and her mother see one another in their dreams thanks to a spell; Georges, on the other hand, is held captive by the Queen's evil spell.

Along with its fantastic adventures, "Abeille" contains a heavy dose of moral admonitions. The central contrast in the story is between the race of men and the race of dwarfs (usually considered physically, hence morally, ugly). The dwarfs are superior in all ways, and humanity is presented as a sorry lot:

> A cela près que, pour donner du prix à la vie de cette race orgueilleuse et misérable, les hommes ont le courage, les femmes la beauté et les petits enfants l'innocence, ô roi Loc, l'humanité toute entière est déplorable ou ridicule. (309-10)

Abeille and Georges combine the innocence of children with their respective adult virtues; and it is by virtue of these qualities, rather than magical means, that they succeed. Georges' honesty and gratitude metaphorically "disarm" King Loc when the dwarf sets him free, and Georges' courage is his only weapon when he comes to rescue Abeille. Similarly, Abeille's generosity and unselfishness (she thrice refuses the offer of the dwarfs' treasure) results in her being crowned Princess of the Dwarfs; and the occasion is marked by a sententious commentary on greed:

> Abeille, les plus beaux trésors seront bien placés entre vos mains. Vous les posséderez et ils ne vous posséderont pas. L'avare est la proie de son or; ceux-là seuls qui méprisent la richesse peuvent être riches sans danger: leur âme sera toujours plus grande que leur fortune.[11]

A contrast with this reward is provided by the old woman's tale which illustrates the punishment of selfishness:

> —Un d'eux vint, par une nuit de décembre, me demander la permission de préparer un grand réveillon dans les cuisines du château.... Il me promit de ne rien égarer ni endommager. Je lui refusai pourtant ce qu'il me demandait, et il se retira en murmurant d'obscures menaces.

---

[11] *Ibid.*, 293. Abeille's innocence in financial matters is prepared by her encounter with a greedy peasant who overcharges her for some cherries: "Abeille prit d'une seule main sa jupe retroussée, tendit de l'autre une pièce d'or à la femme et dit: — Est-ce assez, cela? La paysanne saisit cette pièce d'or, qui eût payé largement toutes les cerises du panier avec l'arbre qui les avait portées et le clos où cet arbre était planté. Et la rusée répondit: — Je n'en demande pas davantage, pour vous obliger, ma petite princesse." (pp. 259-260) It is interesting that the old woman calls Abeille "ma petite princesse." The title endows her with traditional fairy tale credentials and foreshadows her future coronation.

> La troisième nuit, qui était celle de Noël, le même Nain revint dans la chambre où je dormais; il était accompagné d'une infinité d'autres qui, m'arrachant de mon lit, me transportèrent en chemise de nuit sur une terre inconnue.
> —Voilà, dirent-ils en me quittant, voilà le châtiment des riches qui ne veulent point accorder de part dans leurs trésors au peuple laborieux et doux des Nains, qui travaillent l'or et font jaillir les sources. (257)

The conclusion of the old woman's tale indicates the allegorical relationship of the dwarfs (laborious "little" men) with the workers on whom the "sources" of industry depend. The dwarfs preach a kind of christian socialism:

> Soumis comme les Nains à la nécessité de travailler pour vivre, les hommes se sont révoltés contre cette loi divine, et, loin d'être comme nous des ouvriers pleins d'allégresse, ils préfèrent la guerre au travail et ils aiment mieux s'entre-tuer que s'entr'aider. (310)

Mortals, too, advocate compassion; but humanity's capacity for selflessness is limited. Abeille's mother teaches the children respect and devotion to the poor; her attitude is sincere but clearly a traditional attitude of *noblesse oblige*. Even animals provide a moral lesson. As Maurille feeds her hens, she observes:

> Voyez-vous ce gros-là qui mange toute la pitance des petits? Chu! chu! fu! C'est l'image du monde, monseigneur. Tout le bien va aux riches. Les maigres maigrissent, tandis que les gras engraissent. Car la justice n'est point de la terre.[12]

But if justice does not exist on the earth, it is the rule underground in the kingdom of the dwarfs: "C'est la justice, disait Tad, et non la coutume qu'il faut suivre." (273) The story ends with a humanitarian appeal for social harmony:

> Enseignez, en retour, aux enfants que vous aurez, à ne point mépriser les petits hommes innocents et laborieux qui vivent sous la terre. (352)

---

[12] *Abeille*, 336, cf. in "Fanchon": "—Ce n'est point juste, leur dit-elle; il faut que chacun mange à son tour. Elle ne fut point entendue. On n'est guère écouté quand on parle de justice." (France, IV, 10)

All humanity is subject to suffering, and class distinctions disappear before this common bond. The tailor, Jean, comments philosophically on the duchess' sorrow: "C'est ce qui me fait dire que les puissants de ce monde ont aussi leurs peines comme les plus humbles artisans et qu'on connaît à ce signe que nous sommes tous fils d'Adam." (331) Suffering is also to be valued because it renders man capable of pity, the greatest of human virtues:

> Cette vertu, dont la splendeur est pour la pensée ce qu'est pour l'œil le doux éclat des perles, ô roi Loc, c'est la pitié. La souffrance l'enseigne et les Nains la connaissent mal, parce que, plus sages que les hommes, ils ont moins de peines.[13]

France links suffering and pity with love. Abeille finds the dwarfs ugly at first but is told that love will develop compassion; and Georges rejects the pleasures offered by the Nereids for a more human passion: "Je veux retourner où l'on aime, où l'on souffre, où l'on lutte." (321) These relationships are made explicit by King Loc in his concluding homily:

> Mes enfants, ce n'est pas assez de s'aimer beaucoup, il faut encore se bien aimer. Un grand amour est bon, sans doute; un bel amour est meilleur. Que le vôtre ait autant de douceur que de force; que rien n'y manque, pas même l'indulgence, et qu'il s'y mêle un peu de pitié.... On n'aime sûrement que ceux qu'on aime jusque dans leurs faiblesses et leurs pauvretés. Epargner, pardonner, consoler, voilà toute la science de l'amour. (351)

The dwarf's "science" of love is purely emotional, and France's appeal in "Abeille" is to the emotions. He offers the story to those "qui veulent bien qu'on les amuse et dont l'esprit est jeune et joue parfois." (230) In contrast with this suppleness of spirit, science is rigid and devoid of compassion; and for this reason France rejects it in favor of art:

---

[13] *Abeille*, 310, cf. in *Le Jardin d'Epicure*: "La souffrance! quelle divine méconnue! Nous lui devons tout ce qu'il y a de bon en nous, tout ce qui donne du prix à la vie; nous lui devons la pitié, nous lui devons le courage, nous lui devons toutes les vertus." (France, IX, 419)

> La science ne se soucie ni de plaire ni de déplaire. Elle est inhumaine. Ce n'est point elle, c'est la poésie qui charme et qui console. C'est pourquoi la poésie est plus nécessaire que la science. (322)

France criticizes the scientific mentality in "Abeille," but at no time does he parody the scientific method as he does in *Les Sept Femmes*.... He simply deplores the instilling of a dry, scientific mentality in children and treats serious manuals with mock deference:

> J'ai une jolie petite voisine de neuf ans dont j'ai examiné l'autre jour la bibliothèque particulière. J'y ai trouvé beaucoup de livres sur le microscope et les zoophytes, ainsi que plusieurs romans scientifiques. J'ouvris un de ces derniers et je tombai sur ces lignes: "La sèche, *sepia officinalis*, est un mollusque céphalopode dont le corps contient un organe spongieux à trame de chiline associé à du carbonate de chaux." Ma jolie petite voisine trouve ce roman très intéressant. Je la supplie, si elle ne veut pas me faire mourir de honte, de ne jamais lire l'histoire d'*Abeille*. (230-31)

France has couched his own natural science and moral lessons in an agreeable and imaginative form, and this technique is recommended in the text. The dwarfs educate Abeille with entertaining puppets: "Et c'est par des exemples et des spectacles qu'ils lui enseignaient avec une gaieté innocente les curiosités de la nature et les procédés des arts." (287) Georges, too, learns more from his groom, Francoeur, than from his pedantic teachers. The pompous teachers are well-versed in theory, but Francoeur's personal experience and practicality prove to be much more useful. The two "porte-lunettes, le maître d'écriture et le maître de grammaire," are contrasted not only with the naïve groom but with a true scientist, the wise dwarf Nur, whose humble definition of his own wisdom criticizes the pedants indirectly, if not very subtly:

> Roi Loc, répondit Nur, je pourrais savoir beaucoup de choses et n'être qu'un imbécile. Mais je connais le moyen d'apprendre quelques-unes des innombrables choses que

j'ignore, et c'est pourquoi je suis justement renommé comme un savant.[14]

There are elements of parody in "Abeille," but they do not constitute an infrastructure, as in *Les Sept Femmes de la Barbe-Bleue*. To a limited extent, Georges is a parody of the knight errant. Like Parsifal, Georges is characterized by simplicity, and this simplicity is what saves him: "C'était en effet un enfant très simple, et il devait à sa grande simplicité d'avoir échappé aux baisers délicieux et mortels de la reine des Ondines." (325) Georges is compared directly to famous heroes: "il ressemblait plus à Achille parmi les filles de Lycomède qu'à Tannhaüser dans le bourg enchanté." (318) The ideals of chivalry are provided as a model. Georges' father was slain in "combat singulier" and his mother speaks of "ce temps de chevalerie." (235) Georges is inspired by a book he finds in the palace of crystal which:

> traitait de la chevalerie et des dames et on y trouvait contées tout au long les aventures des héros qui allèrent par le monde combattant les géants, redressant les torts, protégeant les veuves et recueillant les orphelins pour l'amour de la justice et l'honneur de la beauté. (321)

Georges' own chivalry gets off to a poor start, however. When he and Abeille are making mud-pies, Georges hits her with the shovel and Francoeur must reprimand him, "Battre les demoiselles n'est pas le fait d'un comte de Blanchelande, monseigneur." (239)

France also parodies literary allusions in his description of Abeille's abduction:

> Abeille, avec ses cheveux d'or répandus sur ses épaules, ressemblait à l'aurore levée sur la montagne, s'il est vrai que parfois l'aurore s'effraye, appelle sa mère et veut fuir, car la fillette en vint à ces trois points.... (280)

---

[14] *Abeille*, 309. Nur lives in the "well of science." The pun is elaborately prepared. First, his cave is called a well: "il prit la résolution de consulter Nur, qui était le plus savant des Nains et habitait au fonds d'un puits creusé dans les entrailles de la terre." (p. 309) Then the well is called a laboratory: "Le roi Loc descendit dans ce puits et trouva Nur dans son laboratoire." (p. 309) It is only after Nur's dissertation on the relative merit of science and poetry that the cliché appears in its entirety: "Au sortir du puits de la science...." (p. 323)

France's technique in this example is similar to the mock heroic; a trivial subject is treated in an elevated manner (the initial comparison of Abeille to the dawn) and the inappropriateness of this comparison is made explicit by the second part of the sentence. A more specific parody can be seen in the countess de Blanchelande's reaction to the white rose: "à cette vue, elle pâlit," (233) which evokes memories of Phèdre in all French readers.

These brief allusions are peripheral to the story, however, and if France makes fun of his protagonists it is neither as fairy tale heroes *per se* or as part of a systematic network of parody.

Another contrast with *Les Sept Femmes...* is provided in France's brief story, "Fanchon," part of the collection of childrens' tales entitled *Nos Enfants* (1886). These stories are not among France's best, and, in fact, when he selected some of the tales in *Nos Enfants* for revision in *Pierre Nozière,* "Fanchon" was not among them. Nevertheless, the story is useful in a comparison of France's use of parody. This story is not a fairy tale; it is a parody of fairy tale heroes. But the parody in "Fanchon" serves no larger purpose and by and large the story is rather insipid. The heroine is a latter-day Red Riding-Hood, minus Red Riding-Hood's adventures:

> Fanchon s'en est allée de bon matin, comme le petit Chaperon rouge, chez sa mère-grand, qui demeure tout au bout du village. Mais Fanchon n'a pas, comme le petit Chaperon rouge, cueilli des noisettes dans le bois. Elle est allée tout droit son chemin et elle n'a pas rencontré le loup.[15]

"Fanchon" is of marginal importance. Along with "Abeille," however, the story does indicate that it is not simply parody but the ironic way in which parody is manipulated which contributes to the interest of the stories in *Les Sept Femmes de la Barbe-Bleue.*

---

[15] France, *Œuvres* (Paris: Calmann-Lévy, 1925), IV, 5.

# SELECTED BIBLIOGRAPHY

Exhaustive bibliographies of works concerning Anatole France can be found in the *Bibliographie des auteurs modernes de langue francaise* by Talvart and Place (V, Paris: Editions de la chronique des lettres françaises, 1935); in Jean Sareil's *Anatole France et Voltaire* (Genève, Droz; Paris, Minard: 1961); or Jean Levaillant's *Les Aventures du scepticisme* (Paris: Armand Colin, 1965). It would serve no useful purpose to reproduce these references, particularly since so little work has been devoted to the stories included in the present study. I have therefore limited my bibliographical references to those works cited or consulted in direct connection with this study.

### A. Works of Anatole France

*Œuvres complètes illustrées*, 25 vols. Carias, L. and Le Prat, G., ed. Paris: Calmann-Lévy, 1925-35.
*La Vie littéraire, cinquième série*. Ed. J. Suffel. Paris: Calmann-Lévy, 1949.
*Vers les temps meilleurs. Trente ans de vie sociale commentés par Claude Aveline*. 4 vols. Paris: Emile-Paul, 1949-1953.
Preface to Hesse, Raymond. *Riquet à la houppe et ses compagnons*. Paris: Mornay, 1923.

### B. Critical Works about Anatole France

Ahlstrom, Alvida. *Le Moyen-Age dans l'œuvre d'Anatole France*. Paris: Société d'Edition les Belles Lettres, 1930.
"The Baptized Penguins: Anatole France's satire on civilization." *Current Literature*, XLVI (1909), 56-59.
"Bee, Princess of the Dwarfs." *Literary Digest*, XLV (1912), 1023.
Bergeret, Lucien. "Anatole France et le plagiat." *L'Opinion*, 23/10/11, pp. 811-12.
Blum, Léon. *En Lisant. Œuvres complètes*, I. Paris: Albin Michel, 1954.
Boillot, Félix. *L'Humour d'Anatole France*, Paris: Les Presses Universitaires, 1933.
Bois, Jules. "Revue des livres." *Les Annales*, 4 juillet, 1909, pp. 6-7.
Braibant, Charles. *Du Boulangisme au Panama: le secret d'Anatole France*. Paris: Denöel et Steele, 1935.
Bresky, Dushan. *The Art of Anatole France*, The Hague, Paris: Mouton, 1969.

## SELECTED BIBLIOGRAPHY

Brousson, Jean-Jacques. *Anatole France en pantoufles.* Paris: Editions G. Crès et Cie., 1926.
Calmettes, Pierre. *La Grande Passion d'Anatole France.* Paris: Editions Seheur, 1929.
Cerf, Barry. *Anatole France.* New York: Dial Press, 1926.
Charpentier, J. L. "Les Variétés du conte moderne." *Revue hebdomadaire,* 26 Sept. 1908, No. 39, pp. 483-500.
Chassé, Charles. *Styles et physiologie.* Paris: Albin Michel, 1928.
Chevalier, Haakon. *The Ironic Temper: Anatole France and his time.* New York: Oxford University Press, 1932.
Coquelin, L. "Les Sept Femmes de la Barbe-Bleue." *Larousse Mensuel,* Sept. 1909, pp. 543-544.
Dargan, Edwin Preston. *Anatole France (1844-1896).* New York: Oxford University Press, 1937.
Esmein, A. "Jeanne d'Arc et son nouvel historien." *Revue politique et parlementaire,* LVIII (11 and 12/08), 295-318; 548-569.
―――. "Encore un historien de Jeanne d'Arc." *Revue Historique,* CII (1909), 62-87.
"France's Masterly Portrayal of Jeanne d'Arc." *Current Literature,* XLV (1908), 68-70.
Jefferson, Carter. *Anatole France: The Politics of Skepticism.* New Brunswick: Rutgers University Press, 1965.
Lang, Andrew. "Le Chef-d'œuvre d'Anatole France." *Fortnightly Review,* LXXXIX (1908), 982-993.
―――. "M. France's *Jeanne d'Arc.*" *Living Age,* CCLVI (1908), 816-819.
Lanson, Gustave. *L'Art de la prose.* Paris: Librairie des annales politiques et littéraires, 1908.
―――. Introduction in Anatole France. *Pages Choisies des auteurs contemporains.* Paris: Calmann-Lévy, 1913.
Latzarus, Louis. "Un Plagiat d'Anatole France." *La Revue Hebdomadaire,* 1/9/23, pp. 98-103.
Lefebvre, Louis. "L'Ironie au temps présent." *Revue Bleue,* 1-8/3/19, pp. 153-56.
Levaillant, Jean. *Les Aventures du scepticisme: essai sur l'evolution intellectuelle d'Anatole France.* Paris: Armand Colin, 1965.
―――. "Aspects de la création littéraire chez France." *Revue d'Histoire littéraire de la France,* Oct.-Nov. 1955, pp. 478-491.
"The Life of Joan of Arc." *Literary Digest,* XL (1910), 239-240.
Luchaire, Achille. "La Jeanne d'Arc d'Anatole France." *Grande Revue,* 25/3/08, pp. 209-234.
Madeleva, Sister M. "Anatole France: Four parodies on historical research." *University of California Chronicle,* XXIX, No. 1 (Jan. 1927), 2-23.
Maurevert, Georges. *Le Livre des plagiats.* Paris: Fayard et Cie, 1922.
Maury, Lucien. "Les Sept Femmes de la Barbe-Bleue." *Revue Bleue,* II (1909), 90-92.
Mériel, E. "L'Italianisme dans l'œuvre d'Anatole France." *Bulletin de l'Université et de l'Académie de Toulouse,* No. 1 (Oct.-Nov. 1944), pp. 1-23.
Monod, G. "La Vie de Jeanne d'Arc." *Revue Historique,* 5-8/08, pp. 410-15.
Mornet, Daniel. "Anatole France et la science." *Revue du mois,* XII (July-Dec. 1911), 60-76.
Nousanne, Henri de. *Anatole France: Philosophe sceptique.* Paris: J. Peyronnet et Cie., 1925.

Peyre, Henri. *L'Influence des littératures antiques sur la littérature française moderne; état des travaux.* Yale Romantic Studies, Vol. XIX. New Haven: Yale University Press, 1941.
Reinach, Salomon. *Cultes, Mythes et Religions,* IV. Paris: Leroux, 1912, pp. 300-322.
Sachs, Murray. *Anatole France: the short stories.* Southampton: The Camelot Press, Ltd., 1974.
———. "Anatole France and the Art of the Short Story." *Kentucky Romance Quarterly,* XX, No. 3 (1973), pp. 359-366.
Sareil, Jean. *Anatole France et Voltaire.* Genève: Droz; Paris: Minard, 1961.
———. "Un Essai plausible de reconstitution historique: *Le Procurateur de Judée* d'Anatole France." *Romanic Review,* LXI, No. 4 (Dec. 1970), 287-295.
Stuffel, Jacques. "La Bibliothèque d'Anatole France." *Le Livre et L'estampe,* No. 5, janvier 1956.
Thibaut, Henri. "La Querelle des sources." *NRF,* 1/11/23, pp. 580-587.
Van Rosebrouck, Gustave. "Sylvestre Bonnard and the Fairy." *Modern Language Notes,* XXXVII (1922), 248-250.
Virtanen, Reino. *Anatole France.* New York: Twayne, 1968.
Woodbridge, B. M. "Sylvestre Bonnard's Fairy Again." *Modern Language Notes,* XXXIX (1924), 380.
Wyndham, Francis. "Anatole France on Joan of Arc." *Dublin Review,* CXLII (1908), 96-109.

C. Works on Fairy Tales, Short Story and General

Aarne, Antti. *The Types of the Folktale,* trans. and enlarg. Stith Thompson. Helsinki, 1964.
Assier, Alexandre. *La Bibliothèque Bleue depuis Jean Oudot 1er jusqu'à M. Baudot, 1600-1863.* Paris: Champion, 1875.
Aulnoy, Madame C. J., Comtesse de. *Les Contes de fées ou fées à la mode.* Vols. II, III and IV of *Le Cabinet des fées.* Amsterdam et Genève, 1785.
Avenel, Joseph de. *Fables, contes, élégies, chansons, épigrammes.* Paris, 1875.
Balzac, Honoré de. *Contes Drolatiques II. Œuvres Complètes,* XXXVII. Paris: Louis Conrad, 1932.
Banville, Théodore de. *Contes Féeriques.* Paris: G. Charpentier, 1882.
Barchilon, Jacques. *Tales of Mother Goose.* New York: Pierpont Morgan Library, 1956.
———. "Uses of the Fairy Tale in the Eighteenth Century." *Studies on Voltaire and the Eighteenth Century,* XXIV (1963), 111-138.
———. "Le Cabinet des fées et l'imagination romanesque." *Etudes littéraires,* I, No. 2 (Aug. 1968), 215-231.
Beauquier, Charles. *Chansons populaires recueillies en Franche-Comté.* Paris: Lechevalier and Leroux, 1894.
Bladé, Jean-François. *Contes populaires de la Gasgogne,* Vol. I, *Contes Epiques.* Les Littératures populaires de toutes les nations, No. 19. Paris: G. P. Maison-Neuve and Larose, 1885; sept. 1967.
Blum, Léon. *Premiers Essais politiques. Œuvres complètes,* I. Paris: Albin Michel, 1954.

# SELECTED BIBLIOGRAPHY

Bossard, Eugène. *Gilles de Rais, maréchal de France*, 2nd. ed. Paris: H. Champion, 1886.
Brémond, Claude. "Le Message narratif." *Communications*, No. 4 (1964), pp. 4-32.
——. "La Logique des possibles narratifs." *Communications*, No. 8 (1966), pp. 60-76.
Bujeaud, Jérôme. *Chants et chansons populaires des provinces de l'ouest.* 2 vols. Paris: Niort, 1895.
*Le Cabinet des fées.* Ed. C. J. Mayer. 41 vols. Amsterdam et Genève, 1785-1789.
Casti, Giovanni Battista. *Novelle di Giambatista Casti.* 3 vols. Parigi: Stamperia Italiana, Anno XII (1804).
Catullus. Ed. Elmer Truesdale Merril. *Catullus.* Cambridge, Mass.: Harvard University Press, 1893.
Cazotte, J. *Les Mille et une fadaises.* Paris, 1742.
Cumings, Edith. *The Literary Development of the Romantic Fairy Tale in France.* Bryn Mawr, 1934.
Daru, Comte P. "Le Roi malade, ou la chemise de l'homme heureux, conte." *Almanach des muses*, XI (1803), 97-100.
Delarue, Paul. *Le Conte populaire français*, I. Paris: Editions Erasme, 1957.
——. "Les Caractères propres du conte populaire français." *La Pensée*, No. 72, Mars-avril, 1957, pp. 40-62.
Deulin, Charles. "Barbe-Bleue." *Revue de France*, XX (Dec. 1876), 975-984.
——. "La Belle au Bois-dormant." *Revue de France*, XX (Dec. 1876), 953-968.
Doutrepont, Georges. *Les Types populaires de la littérature française*, 2 vols. Bruxelles: Albert Dewit, 1926; 1927.
Ducray-Duminil. *Contes de fées.* 4 vols. Paris, 1819.
Dufrenoy, Marie-Louise. *L'Orient romanesque en France: 1704-1789.* 2 vols. Montréal, 1946.
Dupuis, Charles-François. *Origine de tous les cultes ou religion universelle*, édition nouvelle. 3 vols. Paris: Rosier, 1835.
Eberhard, W., and Boratov, P. N. *Typen türkischer volksmärchen.* Wiesbaden, 1953.
Edwards, Paul, ed. *The Encyclopedia of Philosophy.* 6 vols. New York: Macmillan & the Free Press, 1967.
Félice, Ariane de. *Les Techniques du conte traditionnel: essai sur quelques techniques de l'art verbal traditionnel.* Thèse dact. Paris, 1958.
Flowers, Ruth. *Voltaire's Stylistic Transformation of Rabelaisian Satirical Devices.* Washington: The Catholic University of American Press, 1951.
Genlis, Stéphanie Félicité Ducrest de St. Aubin, Comtesse de. *Nouveaux Contes moraux et nouvelles historiques.* 6 vols. *Œuvres*, VII-XII. Paris, 1825.
Girardin, Delphine (Gay). *Contes d'une vieille fille à ses neveux.* 3 vols. Paris: C. Gosselin, 1833.
Gourmont, Rémy de. "Les Contes de fées." *Promenades littéraires.* 1$^{ere}$ Série. Paris: Mercure de France, 1929, pp. 248-257.
Grave, S A. "Some Eighteenth Century Attempts to use the Notion of Happiness." *Studies in the Eighteenth Century*, ed. R. F. Brissenden. Canberra: 1968, pp. 155-169.
Haffter, Pierre. "L'Usage satirique des causales dans les contes de Voltaire." *Studies on Voltaire and the Eighteenth Century*, LIII (1967), 7-28.

Hartland, Edwin Sidney. *The Science of Fairy Tales*. London: Walter Scott, 1891, repr. Detroit: Singing Tree Press, 1968.
Henriot, Emile. *Histoires morales*. Paris: Les Cahiers de Paris, 1925.
Köhler, Reinhold. *Aufsätze über märchen und volkslieder*. Berlin: 1894.
Lafayette, Madame de. *La Princesse de Clèves*. New York: Charles Scribner's Sons, 1930.
Latzarus, Marie Thérèse. *La Littérature enfantine en France dans la seconde moitié du XIX$^e$ siècle*. Paris: Les Presses Universitaires de France, 1924.
Lemaître, Jules. *En Marge des vieux livres, contes*. 2 vols. Paris: Ancienne Librairie Lecène Oudin et Cie, n.d.
Lemirie, Charles. *Un Maréchal et un connétable de France: La Barbe-Bleue de la légende et de l'histoire*. Paris: Ernest Leroux, 1886.
Leprince, de Beaumont, Madame. *La Belle et la bête, magasin des enfants*. Vol. 35 of Le Cabinet des fées. Amsterdam et Genève, 1785.
Lüthi, Max. *Once Upon a Time: on the nature of fairy tales*. New York: Frederick Ungar, 1970.
Mabille, Pierre. *Le Miroir du merveilleux*. Paris: Les Editions de minuit, 1962.
MacGhee, Dorothy. *Fortunes of a Tale: the philosophic tale in France*. Menasha, Wisconsin: G. Banta Publishing Co., 1954.
———. *Voltarian Narrative Devices as considered in the author's contes philosophiques*. Menasha, Wisconsin: G. Banta Publishing Co., 1933.
Mandrou, Robert. *De la Culture populaire aux XVII$^e$ et XVIII$^e$ siècles: la Bibliothèque bleue de Troyes*. Paris: Stock, 1964.
Matthey, Hubert. *Essai sur le merveilleux dans la littérature française depuis 1800*. Paris: Payot, 1915.
Maurois, André. "Le Style de Voltaire." *Europe*, May-June, 1959, pp. 5-6.
———. and Lefèvre, F. "Propos sur le conte philosophique." *Les Nouvelles Littéraires*, 13/11/37.
Maury, Alfred. *Essai sur les légendes pieuses du moyen-âge*. Paris: Lagrange, 1843.
Mauzi, Robert. *L'Idée du bonheur dans la littérature et la pensée françaises au XVIII$^e$ siècle*. Paris: Armand-Colin, 1960.
———. "Les Maladies de l'âme au XVIII$^e$ siècle." *Revue des sciences humaines*, No. 100 (Oct-Nov, 1960), pp. 459-493.
Montégut, Emile. "Des Fées et de leur littérature en France." *Revue des deux mondes*, avril, 1862, pp. 648-675.
Mylne, Vivienne. "Literary Techniques and Methods in Voltaire's *contes philosophiques*." *Studies on Voltaire and the Eighteenth Century*, ed. Theodore Besterman, LVII, 1055-1080.
Nodier, Charles. *Œuvres*. 12 vols. Paris: Renduel, 1832-37.
Offenbach, J. *Barbe-Bleue, opéra bouffe*. Paris: E. Gérard et Cie, 1866.
Paulson, Ronald, ed. *Satire: Modern Essays in Criticism*. Englewood Cliffs, New Jersey: Prentice-Hall, 1971.
Pérès, Jean Baptiste, *Le Grand Erratum*, trans. in Evans, Henry Ridgely, *The Napoleon Myth*. Chicago: The Open Court Publishing Co., 1905.
Propp, Vladimir. *La Morphologie du conte*. Paris: Editions du Seuil, 1965 and 1970.
Rabelais, François, *Œuvres Complètes*. 2 vols. Paris: Garnier Frères, 1962.
Saintyves, P., pseud. for Nourry, Emile. *Les Contes de Perrault et les récits parallèles*. Paris, 1923.

Sand, George. *Les Contes d'une grand'mère*. Paris: Calmann-Lévy, 1892.
Sangiorgi, Roberto Benaglia. "Giambattista Casti's *Novelle Gallanti* and Lord Byron's *Beppo*." *Italica*, No. 28 (1951), pp. 261-69.
Sareil, Jean. *Essai sur Candide*. Genève: Librairie Droz, 1967.
―――. "La Répétition dans les *Contes* de Voltaire." *French Review*, XXXV, No. 2 (Dec. 1961), 137-146.
―――. "De *Zadig* à *Candide,* ou permanence de la pensée de Voltaire." *Romanic Review*, LII, No. 4 (Dec. 1961) 271-278.
Scott, Walter. "The Search After Happiness: or the quest of Sultan Solimaun." *The Complete Poetical Works of Walter Scott*, Cambridge edition. Boston and New York: Houghton Mifflin, 1900.
Sébillot, Paul. *Le Folklore de France*. 4 vols. Paris: 1904.
Storer, Mary Elizabeth. *La Mode des contes de fées* (1685-1700). *Bibliothèque de la revue de littérature comparée*, No. 48. Paris: Librairie Ancienne Honoré Champion, 1928.
Thompson, Stith, ed. *Motif Index of Folk Literature*. 6 vols. Bloomington, Indiana: Indiana University Press, 1955-58.
Todorov, Tzvetan. *Introduction à la littérature fantastique*. Paris: Editions du Seuil, 1970.
Van den Bergh, H. *Giambattista Casti* (1724-1803). Amsterdam and Brussels: Elsevier, 1951.
Vicaire, Gabriel. *Le Miracle de Saint Nicolas*. Paris: Alphonse Lemerre, 1888.
Voltaire. *Œuvres complètes*. 41 vols. Paris: Garnier, 1877-1885.
Walckenaer, Baron Charles Athanase. *Dissertation sur les contes de fées*. Paris, n.d.
Weitzman, Arthur. "The Oriental Tale in the 18th Century: a reconsideration." *Studies on Voltaire and the Eighteenth Century*, LVIII (1967), 1839-55.

# NORTH CAROLINA STUDIES IN THE ROMANCE LANGUAGES AND LITERATURES

I.S.B.N. Prefix 0-8078-

## Recent Titles

CAMUS' HELLENIC SOURCES, by Paul Archambault. 1972. (No. 119). -919-7.

FROM VULGAR LATIN TO OLD PROVENÇAL, by Frede Jensen. 1972. (No. 120). -920-0.

GOLDEN AGE DRAMA IN SPAIN: GENERAL CONSIDERATION AND UNUSUAL FEATURES, by Sturgis E. Leavitt. 1972. (No. 121). -921-9.

THE LEGEND OF THE "SIETE INFANTES DE LARA" (*Refundición toledana de la crónica de 1344* versión), study and edition by Thomas A. Lathrop. 1972. (No. 122). -922-7.

STRUCTURE AND IDEOLOGY IN BOIARDO'S "ORLANDO INNAMORATO," by Andrea di Tommaso. 1972. (No. 123). -923-5.

STUDIES IN HONOR OF ALFRED G. ENGSTROM, edited by Robert T. Cargo and Emmanuel J. Mickel, Jr. 1972. (No. 124). -924-3.

A CRITICAL EDITION WITH INTRODUCTION AND NOTES OF GIL VICENTE'S "FLORESTA DE ENGANOS," by Constantine Christopher Stathatos. 1972. (No. 125). -925-1.

LI ROMANS DE WITASSE LE MOINE. *Roman du treizième siècle*. Édité d'après le manuscrit, fonds français 1553, de la Bibliothèque Nationale, Paris, par Denis Joseph Conlon. 1972. (No. 126). -926-X.

EL CRONISTA PEDRO DE ESCAVIAS. *Una vida del Siglo XV*, por Juan Bautista Avalle-Arce. 1972. (No. 127). -927-8.

AN EDITION OF THE FIRST ITALIAN TRANSLATION OF THE "CELESTINA," by Kathleen V. Kish. 1973. (No. 128). -928-6.

MOLIÈRE MOCKED. THREE CONTEMPORARY HOSTILE COMEDIES: *Zélinde, Le portrait du peintre, Élomire Hypocondre*, by Frederick Wright Vogler. 1973. (No. 129). -929-4.

C.-A. SAINTE-BEUVE. *Chateaubriand et son groupe littéraire sous l'empire*. Index alphabétique et analytique établi par Lorin A. Uffenbeck. 1973. (No 130). -930-8.

THE ORIGINS OF THE BAROQUE CONCEPT OF "PEREGRINATIO," by Juergen Hahn. 1973. (No. 131). -931-6.

THE "AUTO SACRAMENTAL" AND THE PARABLE IN SPANISH GOLDEN AGE LITERATURE, by Donald Thaddeus Dietz. 1973. (No. 132). -932-4.

FRANCISCO DE OSUNA AND THE SPIRIT OF THE LETTER, by Laura Calvert. 1973. (No. 133). -933-2.

ITINERARIO DI AMORE: DIALETTICA DI AMORE E MORTE NELLA VITA NUOVA, by Margherita de Bonfils Templer. 1973. (No. 134). -934-0.

L'IMAGINATION POETIQUE CHEZ DU BARTAS: ELEMENTS DE SENSIBILITE BAROQUE DANS LA "CREATION DU MONDE," by Bruno Braunrot. 1973. (No. 135). -934-0.

ARTUS DESIRE: PRIEST AND PAMPHLETEER OF THE SIXTEENTH CENTURY, by Frank S. Giese. 1973. (No. 136). -936-7.

JARDIN DE NOBLES DONZELLAS, FRAY MARTIN DE CORDOBA, by Harriet Goldberg. 1974. (No. 137). -937-5.

MYTHE ET PSYCHOLOGIE CHEZ MARIE DE FRANCE DANS "GUIGEMAR", par Antoinette Knapton. 1975. (No. 142). -942-1.

THE LYRIC POEMS OF JEHAN FROISSART: A CRITICAL EDITION, by Rob Roy McGregor, Jr. 1975. (No. 143). -943-X.

THE HISPANO-PORTUGUESE CANCIONERO OF THE HISPANIC SOCIETY OF AMERICA, by Arthur Askins. 1974. (No. 144). -944-8.

---

When ordering please cite the *ISBN Prefix* plus the last four digits for each title.

Send orders to: University of North Carolina Press
Chapel Hill
North Carolina 27514
U. S. A.

# NORTH CAROLINA STUDIES IN THE ROMANCE LANGUAGES AND LITERATURES

I.S.B.N. Prefix 0-8078-

## Recent Titles

HISTORIA Y BIBLIOGRAFÍA DE LA CRÍTICA SOBRE EL "POEMA DE MÍO CID" (1750-1971), por Miguel Magnotta. 1976. (No. 145). -945-6.

LES ENCHANTEMENZ DE BRETAIGNE. AN EXTRACT FROM A THIRTEENTH CENTURY PROSE ROMANCE "LA SUITE DU MERLIN", edited by Patrick C. Smith. 1977. (No. 146). -9146-0.

THE DRAMATIC WORKS OF ÁLVARO CUBILLO DE ARAGÓN, by Shirley B. Whitaker. 1975. (No. 149). -949-9.

A CONCORDANCE TO THE "ROMAN DE LA ROSE" OF GUILLAUME DE LORRIS, by Joseph R. Danos. 1976. (No. 156). 0-88438-403-9.

POETRY AND ANTIPOETRY: A STUDY OF SELECTED ASPECTS OF MAX JACOB'S POETIC STYLE, by Annette Thau. 1976. (No. 158). -005-X.

FRANCIS PETRARCH, SIX CENTURIES LATER, by Aldo Scaglione. 1975. (No. 159).

STYLE AND STRUCTURE IN GRACIÁN'S "EL CRITICÓN", by Marcia L. Welles. 1976. (No. 160). -007-6.

MOLIERE: TRADITIONS IN CRITICISM, by Laurence Romero. 1974 (Essays, No. 1). -001-7.

CHRÉTIEN'S JEWISH GRAIL. A NEW INVESTIGATION OF THE IMAGERY AND SIGNIFICANCE OF CHRÉTIEN DE TROYES'S GRAIL EPISODE BASED UPON MEDIEVAL HEBRAIC SOURCES, by Eugene J. Weinraub. 1976. (Essays, No. 2). -002-5.

STUDIES IN TIRSO, I, by Ruth Lee Kennedy. 1974. (Essays, No. 3). -003-3.

VOLTAIRE AND THE FRENCH ACADEMY, by Karlis Racevskis. 1975. (Essays, No. 4). -004-1.

THE NOVELS OF MME RICCOBONI, by Joan Hinde Stewart. 1976. (Essays, No. 8). -008-4.

FIRE AND ICE: THE POETRY OF XAVIER VILLAURRUTIA, by Merlin H. Forster. 1976. (Essays, No. 11). -011-4.

THE THEATER OF ARTHUR ADAMOV, by John J. McCann. 1975. (Essays, No. 13). -013-0.

AN ANATOMY OF POESIS: THE PROSE POEMS OF STÉPHANE MALLARMÉ, by Ursula Franklin. 1976. (Essays, No. 16). -016-5.

LAS MEMORIAS DE GONZALO FERNÁNDEZ DE OVIEDO, Vols. I and II, by Juan Bautista Avalle-Arce. 1974. (Texts, Textual Studies, and Translations, Nos. 1 and 2). -401-2; 402-0.

GIACOMO LEOPARDI: THE WAR OF THE MICE AND THE CRABS, translated, introduced and annotated by Ernesto G. Caserta. 1976. (Texts, Textual Studies, and Translations, No. 4). -404-7.

LUIS VÉLEZ DE GUEVARA: A CRITICAL BIBLIOGRAPHY, by Mary G. Hauer. 1975. (Texts, Textual Studies, and Translations, No. 5). -405-5.

UN TRÍPTICO DEL PERÚ VIRREINAL: "EL VIRREY AMAT, EL MARQUÉS DE SOTO FLORIDO Y LA PERRICHOLI". EL "DRAMA DE DOS PALANGANAS" Y SU CIRCUNSTANCIA, estudio preliminar, reedición y notas por Guillermo Lohmann Villena. 1976. (Texts, Textual Studies, and Translation, No. 15). -415-2.

LOS NARRADORES HISPANOAMERICANOS DE HOY, edited by Juan Bautista Avalle-Arce. 1973. (Symposia, No. 1). -951-0.

ESTUDIOS DE LITERATURA HISPANOAMERICANA EN HONOR A JOSÉ J. ARROM, edited by Andrew P. Debicki and Enrique Pupo-Walker. 1975. (Symposia, No. 2). -952-9.

MEDIEVAL MANUSCRIPTS AND TEXTUAL CRITICISM, edited by Christopher Kleinhenz. 1976. (Symposia, No. 4). -954-5.

---

When ordering please cite the *ISBN Prefix* plus the last four digits for each title.

Send orders to: University of North Carolina Press
North Carolina 27514
Chapel Hill
U. S. A.

# NORTH CAROLINA STUDIES IN THE ROMANCE LANGUAGES AND LITERATURES

I.S.B.N. Prefix 0-8078-

## Recent Titles

SAMUEL BECKETT. THE ART OF RHETORIC, edited by Edouard Morot-Sir, Howard Harper, and Dougald McMillan III. 1976. (Symposia, No. 5). -955-3.

DELIE. CONCORDANCE, by Jerry Nash. 1976. 2 Volumes. (No. 174).

FIGURES OF REPETITION IN THE OLD PROVENÇAL LYRIC: A STUDY IN THE STYLE OF THE TROUBADOURS, by Nathaniel B. Smith. 1976. (No. 176). -9176-2.

A CRITICAL EDITION OF LE REGIME TRESUTILE ET TRESPROUFITABLE POUR CONSERVER ET GARDER LA SANTE DU CORPS HUMAIN, by Patricia Willett Cummins. 1977. (No. 177).

THE DRAMA OF SELF IN GUILLAUME APOLLINAIRE'S "ALCOOLS", by Richard Howard Stamelman. 1976. (No. 178). -9178-9.

A CRITICAL EDITION OF "LA PASSION NOSTRE SEIGNEUR" FROM MANUSCRIPT 1131 FROM THE BIBLIOTHEQUE SAINTE-GENEVIEVE, PARIS, by Edward J. Gallagher. 1976. (No. 179). -9179-7.

A QUANTITATIVE AND COMPARATIVE STUDY OF THE VOCALISM OF THE LATIN INSCRIPTIONS OF NORTH AFRICA, BRITAIN, DALMATIA, AND THE BALKANS, by Stephen William Omeltchenko. 1977. (No. 180). -9180-0.

OCTAVIEN DE SAINT-GELAIS "LE SEJOUR D'HONNEUR", edited by Joseph A. James. 1977. (No. 181). -9181-9.

A STUDY OF NOMINAL INFLECTION IN LATIN INSCRIPTIONS, by Paul A. Gaeng. 1977. (No. 182). -9182-7.

THE LIFE AND WORKS OF LUIS CARLOS LÓPEZ, by Martha S. Bazik. 1977. (No. 183). -9183-5.

"THE CORT D'AMOR". A THIRTEENTH-CENTURY ALLEGORICAL ART OF LOVE, by Lowanne E. Jones. 1977. (No. 185). -9185-1.

PHYTONYMIC DERIVATIONAL SYSTEMS IN THE ROMANCE LANGUAGES: STUDIES IN THEIR ORIGIN AND DEVELOPMENT, by Walter E. Geiger. 1978. (No. 187). -9187-8.

LANGUAGE IN GIOVANNI VERGA'S EARLY NOVELS, by Nicholas Patruno. 1977. (No. 188). -9188-6.

BLAS DE OTERO EN SU POESÍA, by Moraima de Semprún Donahue. 1977. (No. 189). -9189-4.

LA ANATOMÍA DE "EL DIABLO COJUELO": DESLINDES DEL GÉNERO ANATOMÍSTICO, por C. George Peale. 1977. (No. 191). -9191-6.

RICHARD SANS PEUR, EDITED FROM "LE ROMANT DE RICHART" AND FROM GILLES CORROZET'S "RICHART SANS PAOUR", by Denis Joseph Conlon. 1977. (No. 192). -9192-4.

MARCEL PROUST'S GRASSET PROOFS. *Commentary and Variants*, by Douglas Alden. 1978. (No. 193). -9193-2.

MONTAIGNE AND FEMINISM, by Cecile Insdorf. 1977. (No. 194). -9194-0.

SANTIAGO F. PUGLIA, AN EARLY PHILADELPHIA PROPAGANDIST FOR SPANISH AMERICAN INDEPENDENCE, by Merle S. Simmons. 1977. (No. 195). -9195-9.

BAROQUE FICTION-MAKING. A STUDY OF GOMBERVILLE'S "POLEXANDRE", by Edward Baron Turk. 1978. (No. 196). -9196-7.

THE TRAGIC FALL: DON ÁLVARO DE LUNA AND OTHER FAVORITES IN SPANISH GOLDEN AGE DRAMA, by Raymond R. MacCurdy. 1978. (No. 197). -9197-5.

A BAHIAN HERITAGE. An Ethnolinguistic Study of African Influences on Bahian Portuguese, by William W. Megenney. 1978. (No. 198). -9198-3.

TWO AGAINST TIME. *A Study of the very present worlds of Paul Claudel and Charles Péguy*, by Joy Nachod Humes. 1978. (No. 200). -9200-9.

TECHNIQUES OF IRONY IN ANATOLE FRANCE. Essay on *Les sept femmes de la Barbe-Bleue*, by Diane Wolfe Levy. 1978. (No. 201). -9201-7.

---

When ordering please cite the *ISBN Prefix* plus the last four digits for each title.

Send orders to:   University of North Carolina Press
                  Chapel Hill
                  North Carolina 27514
                  U. S. A.

The Department of Romance Studies Digital Arts and Collaboration Lab at the University of North Carolina at Chapel Hill is proud to support the digitization of the North Carolina Studies in the Romance Languages and Literatures series.

www.ingramcontent.com/pod-product-compliance
Lightning Source LLC
Chambersburg PA
CBHW020417230426
43663CB00007BA/1202